THE TOWER BRIDGE,

ITS HISTORY AND CONSTRUCTION FROM THE DATE OF THE EARLIEST PROJECT TO THE PRESENT TIME.

BY

J. E. TUIT, M. Inst. C.E.,

ENGINEER TO SIR WILLIAM ARROL AND CO., THE CONTRACTORS.

1894.

PREFACE.

But little introduction, and no apology, is needed for the publication of this work. The great bridge over the Thames is a structure of such importance, both from a technical point of view and as one of the most conspicuous public works of modern times, that a detailed description of it would seem to be imperatively called for.

The substance of this book has already appeared in the columns of "The Engineer," from the pen of Mr. Tuit, Engineer to Sir William Arrol and Co., but the information there published has been supplemented and brought down to date. The work has been divided into sections, commencing with a review of the early schemes for forming a means of communication between the Middlesex and Surrey banks of the river below London Bridge, followed by a general description of the bridge which has now been built. Detailed descriptions of the Foundations, Superstructure, and Hydraulic Machinery for opening the bridge have been added, and it is believed that the whole will be found to be a complete and accurate history of one of the most important works of this century.

Our thanks are due to Mr. John Wolfe Barry, Vice-President of the Institution of Civil Engineers, and to Sir William Arrol and Co., the contractors, for much valuable assistance.

"Engineer" Office,

   May, 1894.

THE RIGHT HONOURABLE THE LORD MAYOR

(From a Photograph by the London Stereoscopic Company.)

MR. ALDERMAN AND SHERIFF DIMSDALE

(From a Photograph by the London Stereoscopic Company)

THE LORD MAYOR AND SHERIFFS.

A WORK descriptive of one of the most conspicuous public works of modern times would be incomplete without some personal record of the chief officers of the Corporation, to the unaided pecuniary resources of which the public is so heavily indebted. First and foremost amongst them is the Lord Mayor in whose year of office Londoners will be put in full possession of the bridge, which with the expenditure of so much capital and technical skill has been erected for their profit and convenience.

THE RIGHT HONOURABLE THE LORD MAYOR.

The Right Honourable George Robert Tyler was born on 26th August, 1835. He is not the first of his race with City traditions, his father before him having been for many years an energetic and useful member of the Corporation. He was educated privately, and early in life became associated with the firm of which he is now the energetic head. That concern, now known to the world as Venables, Tyler and Son, had its origin upwards of two centuries ago, when one William Venables started a paper mill at Cookham. In 1806 Mr. Venables opened a warehouse in the City of London, at Queenhithe, where the business is still conducted, of which Mr. Alderman Tyler is now the senior partner, and from a date shortly after that time to the present the firm has always contributed working members to the Corporation.

Mr. William Venables, the founder of the firm, was Alderman, Sheriff, and Lord Mayor of London, and for some time represented the City of London in Parliament, and now Lieut.-Colonel T. C. Venables, a partner in the firm, who joined the business about thirty-five years ago, is also a member of the Corporation. Notwithstanding the absorbing calls of business, the Lord Mayor has always found time for the active exercise of those voluntary but none the less responsible duties which our City Governors are called upon to discharge.

He became a member of the Corporation in 1877. In 1887 he was unanimously elected Alderman of the Ward of Queenhithe, and both as civic officer and magistrate he has won universal respect and confidence. He is Master of the Stationers' Company, and a member of the Gold and Silver Wyre Drawers' Company.

MR. ALDERMAN AND SHERIFF MOORE.

MR. ALDERMAN MOORE comes of stout North Country stock. He was born at Stockport in the year 1826. He was educated privately, and at an early age entered the establishment of Messrs. Peek Brothers and Co. of Eastcheap.

In the year 1847 he commenced on his own account, and in 1854 purchased the tea and coffee business originally established in 1823, which he has since so successfully carried on at 35, King William-street, under the style of Moore Brothers, tea merchants. Mr. Alderman Moore is "not afraid to meet his enemy in the gate," for he has seven sons, all of whom are associated with him in the business.

In 1870 he became a member of the Corporation; in 1874 was elected Chairman of the General Purposes Committee; in 1878 Chairman of the Library Committee; and in 1886 Chairman of the Commission of Sewers; and in 1889 was unanimously elected Alderman for the Ward of Candlewick.

His work in the City is only another instance of the great public benefit brought about by individual and voluntary effort. As a member of the Sewers Commission he has been energetic in developing the resources of electricity for lighting purposes, and it was through his action that a Government Inspector was appointed to inspect all consignments of tea to bonded warehouses, with the result that adulteration of this great commodity is now impossible so long as it is under the control of the Customs officials. He has devoted his attention also to the prevention of adulteration of other foods and of drugs, and in this connection has done much useful work. He is Senior Warden of the Loriners' Company, and a member of the Framework Knitters' Company.

MR. ALDERMAN AND SHERIFF DIMSDALE.

Mr. Alderman and Sheriff Dimsdale belongs to a Quaker family. An ancestor accompanied William Penn when he went to Pennsylvania and made his treaty with the Indians. His father—like his predecessor in the Ward of Cornhill, the late Sir R. N. Fowler—was a member of the Society of Friends until middle life; and his aunt, Elizabeth Gurney Dimsdale, is still a member and a minister in the Society.

The Sheriff was born over the Banking House at 49, Cornhill, on January 19th, 1849. He was educated at Eton, and entered the firm of Messrs. Dimsdale, Fowler, Barnard, and Dimsdale, as a partner in 1871. The first of the name in the Bank was Baron Dimsdale, who in the last century travelled to Russia to inoculate the Empress Catherine for small pox, and was created by that Monarch a Baron of the Russian Empire and Councillor of State. The present style of the firm, owing to recent amalgamations, is Prescott, Dimsdale, Cave, Tugwell, and Co., in the management of which the Alderman takes an active part.

Upon the death of the late Alderman Sir R. N. Fowler, Bart., M.P., Mr. Alderman Dimsdale was unanimously elected to succeed him as Alderman for the Ward of Cornhill, in which, as stated above, he was born, and has continuously since actively applied himself to the discharge of his office. His name has long been associated with many public charities:—The London Hospital, the Small Pox Hospital, the London Fever Hospital, the London Orphan Asylum, the Royal Humane Society, the Essex and Herts Medical and Benevolent Society, the Benevolent and Strangers' Friend Society, the Church of England Young Men's Society, and others are indebted to him for active co-operation. He is Hon. Secretary of the City of London Conservative Association, a fellow of the Royal Geographical Society, a member of the Committee of the Institute of Bankers, and an Arbitrator in the Court of Arbitration on Banking. A few days ago he was invested as Grand Treasurer of the Freemasons of England.

He married, in 1873, Beatrice Eliza Bower, only daughter of the late Robert Hunt Holdsworth, Esq., who was a partner in the great sherry house of Messrs. Gonzalez, Byass, and Co., of Xeres and Brabant Court. He has three children living—John Holdsworth, educated at Eton, born 1874, and now learning business habits in the bank ; Beatrice Holdsworth, born 1878 ; and Charlotte May Holdsworth, born 1893. He is a member of the Carlton, Conservative, and City Carlton Clubs.

various parts, is evidence of the increased knowledge of those principles which form the foundation of modern engineering.

EARLY DESIGNS FOR THE TOWER BRIDGE.

The necessity of additional communication across the Thames below London Bridge has long been recognised, and the subject was under the consideration of the authorities of the City and the Metropolitan Board of Works many years ago.

The traffic during twenty-four hours over London Bridge, a bridge only 54ft. wide, taking the average of two days' observations during August, 1882, was 22,242 vehicles, and 110,525 pedestrians, a number of people equivalent to one-half of the population of such a city as Edinburgh.

Although there exists great difference of opinion regarding the best method of providing additional facilities for crossing the river, yet all authorities have long been agreed that, however the problem was solved, whether by constructing a bridge or a tunnel, there was no site offering so many advantages as the one which has been chosen, the northern approach being immediately to the east of the Tower of London, and the southern approach a little to the west of Horselydown Stairs—see map, Fig. 18.

The various ways by which a communication between the two sides of the river can be effected are as follows:—(1) A low-level bridge, with an uninterrupted roadway; (2) a low-level bridge, with an opening for vessels through it; (3) a high-level bridge, with inclined road approaches; (4) a high-level bridge, with hydraulic lifts; (5) a tunnel under the river, with inclined approaches; (6) a tunnel with hydraulic lifts; (7) a ferry.

There can be no doubt that as far as the road traffic is concerned, a low-level fixed bridge would be the most suitable. The ascents and descents which are unavoidable in the case of a high-level bridge or tunnel are not necessary, and the approaches that are needed would not be costly; but such a bridge would prevent the passage under it of most of the masted vessels which at present navigate up to the wharves as far as London Bridge, and such interference would entail a heavy payment for compensation to those wharfingers and other persons directly and indirectly interested. If a bridge of this kind were built, the river traffic would, however, probably accommodate itself in a great measure to the new condition. A low-level bridge with an opening in the centre, while having many of the advantages above described, would also permit of the river traffic being carried on.

One of the principal objections to this scheme is the difficulty of navigating vessels of any size through the opening portion of the bridge. The Engineer to the Thames Conservators stated in 1877 that "a low-level bridge, with a headway not less than that of London Bridge, if provided with means of transit through it, would be objectionable on account of the obstruction to the navigation that would be involved. In order to pass it, every ship coming up with the flood tide, or going down on the ebb, would have to be brought up head upon tide, made fast to a buoy, and then veered through the openings of the bridge, an operation not always easy of accomplishment, especially during the prevalence of strong winds. To carry out this operation the whole space between the tiers of ships on either side of the river would, for the time being, be occupied, occasioning great disturbance and obstruction to the passing traffic. To make the side arches or openings available for the passage of vessels, some probably three or four of the tiers of ships and barges must be abolished. At present the maintenance of those tiers appears essential for the business of the adjoining wharves; not merely of those to the westward, but also for those to the eastward of the bridge. Whether the interests of the navigation do or do not outweigh the public requirements for bridge accommodation, would have to be considered after the wharfingers and others interested had had an opportunity of stating their case."

The objection to a high-level bridge is the length and inclination of its approaches. If such a bridge was provided with platforms at either end, upon which the road traffic could be raised and lowered by hydraulic lifts with great rapidity, the cost of forming the approaches would be saved; but it is not certain that the traffic could be dealt with thus in a satisfactory manner. And even if it were, the cost of maintenance of such a structure would be the source of considerable expense.

A tunnel under the river would, when once constructed, avoid any interference with the navigation, but vehicular traffic would have to pass nearly a mile, and pedestrians nearly half a mile under ground, and the approaches to it on the north side would be circuitous. Its inclination would vary from 1 in 36 to 1 in 43, and its ascents and descents would be the same in the aggregate as those for a bridge having a clear headway of 85ft. above high water.

The maintenance of a tunnel is generally a very heavy expense, and if hydraulic lifts were substituted for the rising approaches, such expense would be considerably increased, although the cost of constructing the approaches would be saved.

The experience that has been gained in the construction of subaqueous tunnels shows that they are to be avoided wherever possible. The time needed to carry out such works, and their ultimate cost, are, in nearly all cases, unknown quantities when the undertakings are commenced. The Severn Tunnel, which is a little over four miles in length, is by far the most important subaqueous work yet accomplished, but it took no less than thirteen years to complete it, and the cost greatly exceeded the original estimate. The tunnel under the Mersey, which is only one mile in length between the pumping shafts, took some six years to construct. Some idea of the cost of pumping alone that is sometimes necessary during such work may be formed from the fact that the pumping power provided in the case of the Severn Tunnel was sufficient to fill a tank one square mile in area to a depth of 15ft. in twenty-four hours.

Even when such schemes are successfully accomplished, the accommodation offered for traffic is very limited compared to that which would have been afforded by a bridge. In the tunnel now being constructed under the Thames at Blackwall, the width of the roadway, including two 3ft. footpaths, is only 22ft.; and although but about one-half of the total length of one and one-sixth miles is really a tunnel, the estimated cost of the work is nearly £900,000, to which sum it is necessary to add the cost of the property and land required.

With regard to ferries, it must be admitted that they, however well organised, can never be made an efficient

(19)

Fig. 1—DESIGN FOR BRIDGE NEAR THE TOWER BY MR. (NOW SIR) GEORGE BARCLAY BRUCE, 1878

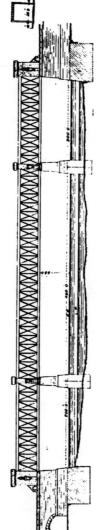

Fig. 2—DESIGN FOR TOWER BRIDGE BY SIR JOSEPH BAZALGETTE, 1878

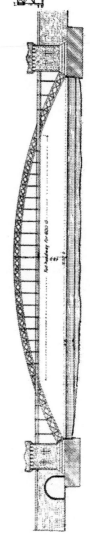

Fig. 3—ALTERNATIVE DESIGN BY SIR JOSEPH BAZALGETTE, 1878

(21)

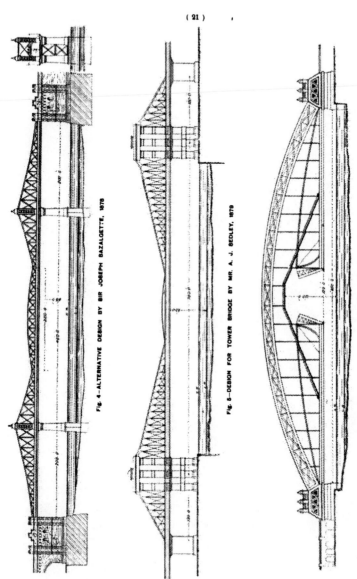

Fig. 4—ALTERNATIVE DESIGN BY SIR JOSEPH BAZALGETTE, 1878

Fig. 6—DESIGN FOR TOWER BRIDGE BY MR. A. J. BEDLEY, 1879

Fig. 7—DESIGN FOR TOWER BRIDGE BY MESSRS, ORDISH AND MATHESON, 1885

(28)

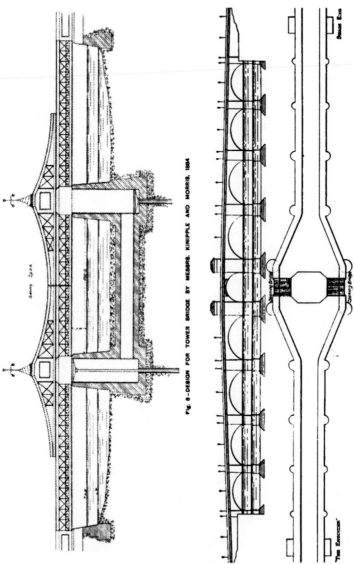

Fig. 6—DESIGN FOR TOWER BRIDGE BY MESSRS. KINIPPLE AND MORRIS, 1884

Fig. 12—DESIGN FOR BASCULE OPENING BRIDGE OVER THE THAMES BY GENERAL BENTHAM, 1901

"The Engineer"

(25)

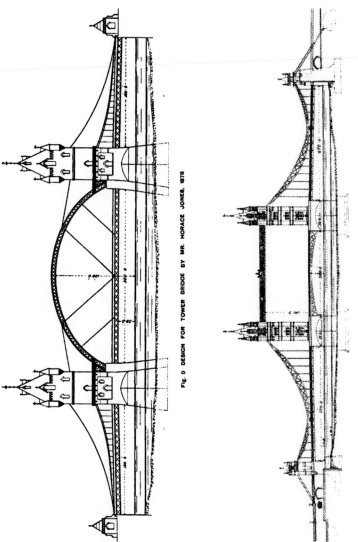

Fig. D DESIGN FOR TOWER BRIDGE BY MR. HORACE JONES, 1878

Fig. 11—GENERAL VIEW OF COMPLETED TOWER BRIDGE, MR. JOHN WOLFE BARRY, ENGINEER

substitute for an uninterrupted line of communication such as is provided by a bridge. The ferry system of New York is carried on under the most favourable conditions, and at great expense, by a vast number of large boats which convey the road and railway traffic across the East River and Hudson River, to Brooklyn, Long Island, and Jersey City. The most important of these is the Fulton Ferry, between New York and Brooklyn, which carries 1,100,000 vehicles and 22,000,000 foot passengers annually. Still, after half a century's experience, it has been found impossible to meet the demands of public convenience by such means, and both bridges and tunnels are, in consequence, either in course of construction or have been already built. A ferry would always be subject to interruption in times of frost and fog. At the last annual meeting of the London and Tilbury Lighterage Company it was stated that during the year there were twenty-seven days on which work was more or less suspended on the river owing to fog; and

during the three years 1879 to 1881 there were on the average thirty-eight days on which fogs were so dense that the South-Eastern Railway Company could not work its trains between Cannon-street and Charing Cross without using fog signals and experiencing delays. To this should be added twelve days of frost, making fifty days in the year on which ferries would be unable to work. For the last two winters, during the construction of the Tower Bridge, it has been impossible to row across the river for weeks together, on account of accumulations of floating ice.

An attempt was made in 1877 by the Thames Steam Ferry Company to deal with the traffic across the river. The site selected for the ferry was directly over the Thames Tunnel, one and a-half miles east of London Bridge. A great advantage of this site was that no vessels are allowed to moor within a certain distance of the line of the tunnel, therefore the ferry boats would have a clearer course here than could be obtained at any other part of the river. The ferry was designed of sufficient capacity to

convey twelve two-horse wagons each way, in addition to foot passengers, every fifteen minutes; and although a considerable sum was expended on its construction, it nevertheless was only in operation for a few years. The traffic had to be raised and lowered in accordance with the state of the tide, and hydraulic lifts, 70ft. long by 35ft. wide, were provided for this purpose on each side of the river. This is one of the few instances where vehicular traffic has been dealt with by means of hydraulic hoists. Another example is to be found in the ferry over the Mersey at Seacombe, which was opened in 1880. In this case there are two hydraulic hoists, each 28ft. long by 9½ft. wide, with a maximum lift of 89½ft. Soon after it was opened this ferry carried 28,000 passengers across the river in one day.

From what has already been said, it is evident that considerable difficulty must be experienced in deciding on the best method of forming a roadway between the two banks of the Thames at this point. As a similar problem

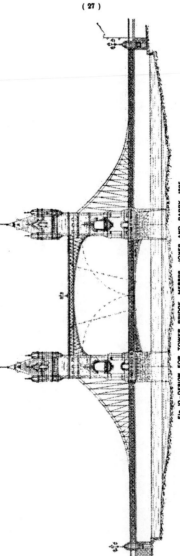

Fig. 10—DESIGN FOR TOWER BRIDGE, MESSRS. JONES AND BARRY, 1885

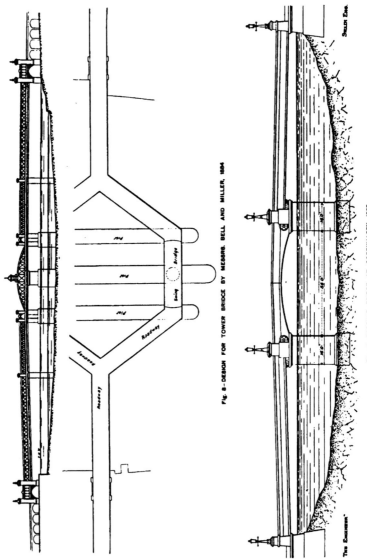

Fig. 8—DESIGN FOR TOWER BRIDGE BY MESSRS. BELL AND MILLER, 1884

Fig. 13—BASCULE BRIDGE AT COPENHAGEN, 1889

has often to be solved for other large cities, it will be interesting to shortly examine the various schemes that have been proposed in the present case, before the design which has now been carried out was finally selected.

In February, 1867, Colonel Haywood, engineer to the City Commissioners of Sewers, recommended the crossing of the Thames by a bridge situated on the east side of the Tower, and in May, 1877, the City Architect reported to his Bridge Committee on the main features of high and low level bridges, as well as on a subway under the Thames, and recommended the site now chosen as being the most favourable for these projects. In 1878, the City Architect advocated a low-level bridge, with a central opening on the bascule principle, as most suitable for crossing the river at this point.

Some two years before this, however, Mr. G. Barclay

manner be propelled over to the opposite shore, when it would discharge its load.

The weight of the whole moving structure, when fully loaded between the guard gates at each end with 1½ cwt. per square foot, was estimated at 5000 tons, and the total cost, including piers and machinery, at £144,000. Mr. Bruce's estimate of the capacity of the bridge was 100 vehicles and 1400 passengers at each crossing, which was to take only three minutes; and he considered that the working expenses would not exceed £10,000 per annum.

In 1877 Mr. Henry Vignoles proposed a mean level bridge which was to consist of three spans, each 300ft., formed of lattice girders. The roadway was to have a clear width of 60ft., and 85ft. of head-room at low-water was allowed for vessels in the middle of the stream, and 76ft. at the abutments of the bridge. With regard to the

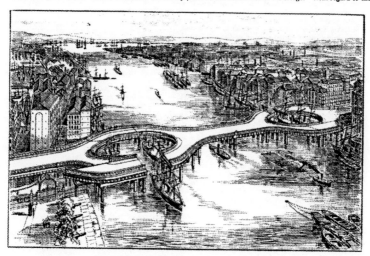

DESIGN FOR TOWER BRIDGE BY MR. F. J. PALMER. 1877

Bruce proposed a rolling bridge, which was to consist of a platform 300ft. long by 100ft. wide, carried by six piers placed in the river about 100ft. apart—Fig. 1. On each of these piers was to be placed a series of rollers, and the necessary machinery for propelling the platform from shore to shore. By such an arrangement the clear waterway of 700ft. was secured. The movable platform, being 300ft. long, would always be supported by at least two piers, and when at either end of its travel it would take a bearing on one of the abutments of the bridge, and as soon as it was loaded with passengers and vehicles the shafts on which the rollers were mounted, being set in motion by machinery in the piers, would cause it to move forward, until it began to take a bearing upon the rollers of the next pier. The rollers of this pier would then be set in motion, and the platform would in this

approaches, one of the peculiar features of this design was the method proposed for overcoming the difficulties of that on the south side of the river. This was to be accomplished by the erection of a gigantic warehouse about 750ft. long and 100ft. wide, along the sides and ends of which the approach road was to rise to the bridge level by the easy gradient of 1 in 50. The warehouse was to be placed along the bank of the river, there being direct access from its various floors to the approach which passed round the building, and the whole of the river front was to be available for wharfage accommodation, while almost the whole of the area occupied by the approach could be utilised as warehouse space. The erection of the warehouse would have, it was believed, recouped to a great extent the cost of land. The approach on the north side of the river would rise to the level of the bridge by a gradient of 1 in 47. The estimated cost of this bridge, warehouse, and approaches, exclusive of the purchase of property, was £800,000.

Early in 1878 Sir Joseph Bazalgette, engineer to the Metropolitan Board of Works, recommended the building of a bridge having a clear headway of 65ft. above Trinity high-water, and in the following session the Board applied to Parliament for power to construct such a bridge. The Bill, however, did not receive the sanction of the House, it being strongly opposed, chiefly because the headway allowed for passing vessels was considered too little, and also on account of the nature of the approach to the bridge on the south side of the river, which it was proposed should be in the form of a spiral about 800ft. in diameter—see Fig. 14, Plate I. The inclination of the approaches was to be 1 in 50 to 60 on the north side, and 1 in 40 on the south side of the river. Three different designs were made for this bridge, see Figs. 2, 3, and 4, and Plates I. and II. Two were for bridges of three spans, with two piers placed in the river in the line of the present tiers of shipping, so as to give a clear width of navigable waterway in the centre of the river of 444ft., and two side openings of 184ft. each; the other design was for a bridge having a clear span of 850ft. across the river.

It was intended to make the width of the bridge 60ft., subdivided into two footways of 12ft. each, and a carriageway of 36ft. The bridge would therefore have been 6ft. wider than London Bridge. The single span of 850ft. was to be a braced arch bridge, having a rise of 106ft., the roadway being partly above and partly below its soffit. The estimated cost was one and a-quarter million, or about £150,000 more than the three-span bridge.

As this scheme was opposed on account of the headroom being too little for vessels navigating the river, Sir Joseph Bazalgette proposed an alternative design in 1882 for a high-level bridge with a clear headway of 85ft. above Trinity high-water, crossing the river by an arch in the same way as he suggested in 1878, but having improved and straight approaches on the south side, and he estimated the probable cost of such a structure to be nearly two millions. The question of the minimum headway for vessels that could be allowed was one of great importance. According to the return of the wharfingers, proved before the Committee on the Tower Bridge Bill in 1878, there were then fifteen pole-masted vessels navigating to the wharves, the masts of which would have to be altered to allow them to pass under a bridge which only gave 65ft. clear headway above high water. There were sixty-three vessels which would have to lower their topmasts, and these seventy-eight vessels make 385 journeys during the year. By raising the headway of the bridge from 65ft. to 85ft., the number of vessels having to lower their top-masts would be reduced from six to one per day.

Although Sir Joseph Bazalgette was always in favour of a high-level bridge, he nevertheless submitted plans to the Metropolitan Board of Works for various other projects, and his approximate estimates for such were as follows :—

A low-level bridge with approaches :—

	£
Cost of works	490,000
Cost of lands	240,000
Cost of compensation	2,250,000
Total cost	2,980,000

A low-level opening bridge :—

	£
Cost of works	570,000
Cost of lands	240,000
Cost of compensation	1,250,000
Total cost	2,060,000

A tunnel with approaches :—

	£
Cost of works	1,110,000
Cost of lands	755,000
Total cost	1,865,000

A high-level bridge with 85ft. headway :—

	£
Cost of works	780,000
Cost of lands, &c.	1,065,000
Total cost	1,845,000

A high-level bridge with 100ft. headway with hydraulic hoists :

	£
Cost of works	670,000
Cost of lands	75,000
Working expenses capitalised	450,000
Total cost	1,195,000

The working expenses being taken as varying from £12,000 to £23,000 per annum, say, £18,000, which capitalised at 4 per cent., amounts to £450,000.

Besides these new works he considered a proposal for widening London Bridge, and he estimated that the necessary alterations and additions to that structure would cost:—

To widen London Bridge :—

	£
Cost of works	375,000
Cost of lands	830,000
	1,205,000

In 1879 Mr. A. J. Sedley proposed a high-level bridge—Fig. 5. This structure was to have a clear span of 750ft., and two side spans of 150ft. each. The clear headway above low water was 85ft., and the side spans were on a gradient of 1 in 50. The total width of the bridge was 60ft. The large span was composed of two cantilevers each 300ft. long, between the ends of which was a central girder 150ft. in length. The approach on the north side of the river was to be on a gradient of 1 in 50, and it was proposed that it should be carried on columns and girders so as to interfere as little as possible with the property through which it passed. On the south side a spiral approach was to be adopted, having a gradient also of 1 in 50. One of the principal features of this bridge was, that it would have been possible to construct it without any staging in the river, by what is known as the overhang system of erection.

The estimated cost of the work was £47,500 for foundations and piers, and about £140,000 for the superstructures ; the approximate total cost, including the purchase of land, being £600,000.

In 1883 the London Chamber of Commerce having announced that it was prepared to exhibit in its Council Rooms any maps, plans, or models of bridges, tunnels, or other proposed means of communication across the Thames below London Bridge, or to receive any communications bearing upon the subject, whether for or against the various projects, obtained particulars of eleven schemes, among the principal of which were the following : A design exhibited by Messrs. Maynard and Cooke for what they called a high-level tunnel, the roof of which was not to be much below the present bed of the river, so that no hydraulic lifts would be required at the ends, and the difficulty of long and steep approaches would consequently be removed. This tunnel was to have been built on the shore, in 60ft. lengths of wrought iron plates and arched ribs, similar to a ship, and it was proposed to line it with a brick and concrete casing from 3½ft. to 8ft. thick. Inside the casing a roadway 88ft. wide and two footways 8½ft. wide were to be provided. As each length was completed on the shore it was proposed to close its ends, and float it out until it was vertically over its destined position. It was then to have been lowered to the bed of the river, and sunk to its final place, as a caisson. The estimated cost of the work was £458,000.

Mr. C. T. Guthrie exhibited designs for a steam ford, similar to the system in use at Saint Malo. Rails were to be laid on a level surface prepared across the river

Passengers and vehicles during this time would be lowered to, and raised from, the level of the subway by means of hydraulic hoists. The clear headway above high water when the swinging span is closed is shown in this design to be 29ft. A special feature of the swinging span is that the tail ends or counterweights would swing clear of the top of the fixed portion of the bridge. The estimated cost of such a bridge was £500,000.

In May, 1885, Messrs. R. M. Ordish and Ewing Matheson published a description of a bridge for crossing the river at the site of the newly-erected bridge. They state in their report on the work that as " no opportunity was afforded to bridge engineers to submit designs to the Corporation, they propounded the following scheme for

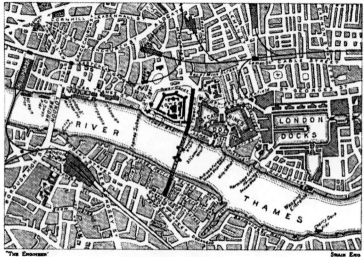

FIG. 18—MAP OF DISTRICTS CONNECTED BY THE TOWER BRIDGE

bed, upon which a framework of wheels was to run. This framework carried a number of columns, all braced together and surmounted by a platform situated at the level of the landing stages. Upon this platform an engine was placed for driving the wheels below. The platform received its vehicles and passengers on one side of the river, and then steamed across with them to the opposite shore.

In 1884 Messrs. Kinipple and Morris submitted to the trustees of the Bridge House Estates a design for a low-level bridge of three spans, the central one, which opened, being 250ft. long—Fig. 6. By means of shafts down each pier, communication was to be effected with a subway underneath the bed of the river, so that traffic could be continuously maintained when the central span was opened to allow the passage of vessels through the bridge.

the consideration of those concerned." Fig. 7 and the following explanation show the kind of structure they proposed in order to carry out the suggestions recommended in the report of a Parliamentary Committee of 1884—of a low-level bridge with mechanical openings. They have not followed that part of the report of the Committee which recommends two openings of 100ft., with a pivot bridge revolving on one central pier, because, in their opinion, any fixed pier in the river is to be avoided, and also because the moving part of such a bridge would present too great an obstruction. They therefore proposed another method of providing a mechanical opening, and in making their design were guided by the following conditions:—

(1) That the roadway should be of ample width and moderate gradients. Provision is therefore made for four

lines of vehicles and two footpaths, each 9ft. wide, the gradient on the bridge being 1 in 100. The northern approach would either be made level or with ascending and descending gradients from the Minories, as proposed by the Corporation. The approach on the Surrey side would be inclined 1 in 40.

(2) In order that the waterway of the river should not be impeded, they suggested that the bridge should be of one span, so that no piers whatever are needed in the river.

(3) So that masted vessels could pass through the bridge, a mechanical opening 120ft. wide is provided, giving a headway of 120ft. above high water.

(4) Not only should the bridge when built present the minimum obstruction to the waterway, but obstruction during the process of building should also be avoided as much as possible. At all the bridges hitherto constructed over the river Thames at London, the staging, coffer-dams, and other temporary works have occupied a considerable portion of the waterway, impeding the movement of river craft to a great extent; and in the case of the Tower Bridge proposed by the Corporation, this obstruction would probably last for two or three years at least, and would be even a greater obstruction than the bridge itself when finished. In the design under consideration, the building of the bridge without any such temporary structures is provided for; except coffer-dams at each shore, projecting about 10ft. into the stream.

(5) Being of opinion that it is not only probable, but almost certain, that in a few years' time the course of trade upon the river, and the inconveniences that must attend even the best kind of opening, will together cause the disuse of the moving part of the bridge, they consider that this contingency should not be lost sight of in any bridge to be built now; and the design here described is for a bridge which will conveniently allow, if the time should ever arrive, of alteration to a closed structure and unbroken roadway.

(6) That in a few years' time there may be a demand which, in the public interest, will have to be accorded, for a railway crossing below London Bridge. The design here put forward shows a structure of sufficient strength and width for the addition of four lines of railway.

Messrs. Ordish and Matheson proposed to construct the bridge in one span of 850ft., with four main ribs or arches of wrought iron or steel. The thrust of the arches would be taken on masonry abutments built on concrete foundations on the London clay, which is well suited to sustain such a load.

The roadway would be suspended from the arched ribs by vertical members strongly braced together, and in the centre a portion of the roadway would be movable, and made to hinge upward as a bascule bridge, leaving an opening 120ft. wide and 120ft. high for vessels to pass through. If, however, it were deemed important to provide a wider opening than here proposed, the design would admit of one 150ft., or even 200ft. in width.

In regard to the future addition of a railway, which is contemplated in the design, it is proposed to carry the four lines of rails above the road traffic, this higher-level being as necessary for railways as the low level is for the street traffic.

It was proposed to erect this bridge as follows:—On either shore of the river suitable staging would be erected

to carry a half span of one pair of ribs. By means of a sufficient counterweight at the shore end, the overhanging weight of the ribs could be balanced, and the staging could then be removed. The half arches could then be propelled forward over the river on a suitable cradle, resting on the approaches, till they met the corresponding half arches which had been similarly erected on the other shore. These half arches would of course meet over the middle of the stream, and could then be united. The second pair of ribs could then be erected in the same way, and afterwards braced to the first pair. During the interruption to the road traffic, while the bridge is open for masted vessels, foot passengers would be able to cross by stairs attached to the outside of the main ribs, as shown in the figure. The opening portion of the bridge would be worked by hydraulic power.

The bridge as here proposed was estimated to cost in the first instance, that is to say as a road bridge with a mechanical opening, and without railways, but with sufficient strength to carry such hereafter, £820,000. This sum includes the bridge, the abutments, the approaches, in fact everything except cost of land and compensation. The cost of altering the structure to a closed bridge, and of adding four lines of railway, is estimated at £45,000 exclusive of the railway approach viaducts. If the bridge were only made sufficiently strong to carry the road traffic, without any provision being made for the railways, the cost would be reduced to about £600,000.

In 1884 the Metropolitan Board of Works, having failed to obtain the approval of Parliament to their high-level bridge scheme of 1879, brought before the House a Bill for power to construct subways under the river, a little to the eastward of the site which they had proposed for the bridge. There were to be two subways side by side, one for carriage traffic and one for pedestrians. Sir Joseph Bazalgette stated in his evidence in support of the scheme, that the total length of the covered way under the river would be 1100ft., or about one-fifth of a mile; the subway for vehicles would be 36ft. wide, 17ft. in height, and 5ft. thick, while the width of that for foot passengers would be 12ft., and its height 14ft. It was ultimately proposed, however, to increase the headway to 18¾ft. at the centre and 14½ft. at the sides of the larger tunnel. The approaches to the carriage subway on the north side of the river would have an inclination of 1 in 25½, and on the south side 1 in 40 up to the place where it was intended that hydraulic lifts should be situated, and the remainder 1 in 27. The approaches to the smaller subway would be on a gradient of 1 in 25 on both sides of the river, and the length of these, including the subway, would be 2200ft. At the deepest part the roadways would be 60ft. below high water. The subways would be constructed by means of coffer-dams extending into the river 150ft. from the north and 218ft. from the south shore, and it would take twelve months to complete this section of the work. When it was finished these dams would be removed and others made 188ft. further into the river on the north side, and 218ft. on the south side, and when this portion of the subway was built, which he anticipated would be in ten months, these dams would be removed and the work extended from the southern end only, by a dam 208ft. long, and the remaining length of 208ft. would be executed in a similar manner. If it were to take eighteen months to finish the work in these last two dams, the time occupied

Fig. 75—VIEW FROM THE SOUTH-WEST, MARCH, 1893

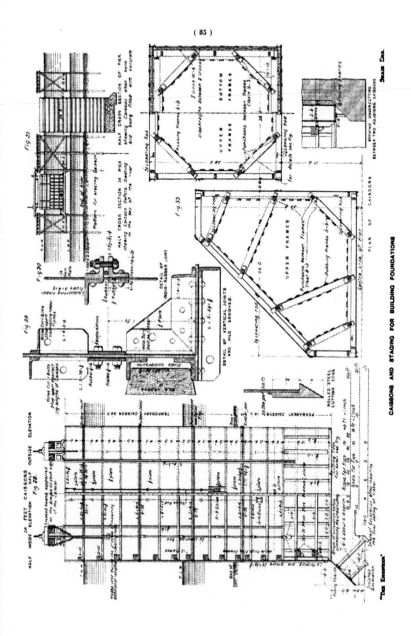

CAISSONS AND STAGING FOR BUILDING FOUNDATIONS

to complete the whole scheme would be three years and four months. There were to be six hydraulic lifts, five of which would average 50ft. long, while one would be 60ft., and all would be 11½ft. wide. It was proposed to provide two additional lifts on the north side to lower the heavy traffic, as the gradient on that side was rather steeper than on the other. The amount of heavy traffic that could be accommodated was estimated at 450

The sum of £500,000 was to be paid out of the £950,000 to the London and St. Katherine Dock Company, in respect for lands and warehouses taken for the purpose of widening Nightingale-lane.

The cost of working the lifts was stated to be £8000 per annum, which sum, if capitalised, would add a considerable amount to the first cost of the scheme.

A large amount of evidence was given regarding the

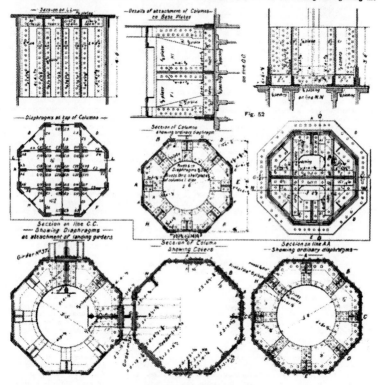

Fig. 22a—SECTIONS OF MAIN COLUMNS

vehicles at each end per hour, or about one-half of that of the same description passing over London Bridge.

It was considered the cost of the project would amount to £1,900,000, this sum being made up as follows:—

Cost of northern approaches	£219,000
Cost of southern approaches	206,000
Cost of subways	380,000
Cost of hydraulic apparatus	100,000
Contingencies	45,000
Cost of lands	950,000
Total cost	1,900,000

proposed hydraulic lifts, and the probable effect such would have on the horses using them. Mr. Falconer, who for some time had charge of the Thames Steam Ferry, said the lifts connected with that undertaking were raised and lowered various heights according to the state of the tide, the maximum range being a little over 28ft. They were 80ft. long and 45ft. wide, the weight of each was eighty tons, and the maximum load fifty tons. On one occasion there were as many as eight two-horse drays, and one or two smaller vehicles on the lift, and the time occupied in placing them thereon was two minutes. In June, 1881, over 7000 horses and 5000 vehicles used the ferry, the working expenses of which averaged about £100 per week.

A carman also gave evidence that he, with a team of three horses, had frequently used the lifts, and had never experienced any inconvenience, the animals took no notice of being raised and lowered, and were as quiet as when in their stables.

This subway scheme was, however, finally rejected, because, in the opinion of the Committee, " sufficient accommodation was not provided for the traffic, the relief of which the subway was intended to effect."

A design for the present London Bridge was proposed by General Bentham, Inspector-General of the Naval Works of the Admiralty, and was published in 1801 in the report of a select committee upon the improvement of the port of London.

This bridge, Fig. 12, was " designed to exemplify a mode of admitting ships to pass through it at all times without occasioning any interruption to the land communication over it." The bridge was considerably widened where the opening portion occurred, the roadway over which was formed by two movable platforms, placed some distance apart, one of which it was intended should always be in position for the road traffic, even while a vessel was passing through the bridge. It has several times been proposed to adopt this principle for a bridge over the Thames below London Bridge. In 1876 Mr. Barnett patented this form of structure, and suggested that such a bridge should be built across the river just below the Tower. The leading features of this bridge were identical with those of General Bentham's design, and will be found in the " Journal of the Society of Arts." In the following year Mr. F. I. Palmer proposed a somewhat similar bridge for the same site, and in order to lessen the great difficulty that would be experienced in navigating ships through the opening of the bridge during strong tides, he suggested that two openings should be provided, each of which were to be placed in the slack tide-way, near either shore, leaving the centre of the river clear for the above-bridge traffic—See page 29.

In 1884 Messrs. Bell and Miller introduced a Bill into Parliament for a bridge over the Thames also at the same site. This duplex bridge, as it was called—Fig. 8 —was in principle the same as that suggested in 1801.

Commencing from the shore, the bridge was to have an ordinary span of about 210ft. on either side of the river, but at the end of this span the roadway becomes duplicated, and the two portions diverge from each other over a span of 100ft. measured on the square. In the middle of the stream there were to be two opening spans of 50ft. clear, but ultimately it was proposed to increase these spans to 60ft., and the diverging roadways were to be connected to those on the opposite shore by swing bridges. By this arrangement it was contended there would be no interruption to vehicular or pedestrian traffic. A ship coming up or down stream would pass the first swing bridge, which would then be closed behind it, before the one in front of it was opened; the operation being very similar to going through a lock. The headway under the swing bridges was to have been 29ft., but this was to be gradually reduced until at the abutments it would be 20½ft.

The gradients of the approaches varied from 1 in 33 to 1 in 130; they were to have a 34ft. roadway, and two footpaths, each 8ft. wide, but on the bridge the roadway and footpaths were reduced to 28ft. and 7ft. respectively.

The estimated cost of the works was £280,000, and a further sum of £68,175 was required for the purchase of the land. The estimates were not, however, regarded by the Committee as sufficient, and they were subsequently increased to £298,000 and £107,000 respectively. This Bill shared the same fate as that for the Metropolitan Board of Works subway scheme, and the Select Committee who rejected these proposals made a special report upon the subject, in which they stated they were unanimously of opinion that upon various grounds they could not recommend that the Duplex Bridge Bill should be passed, neither did they feel warranted in recommending the expenditure of two millions of public money for the construction of the subways, which could at best be regarded as a compromise, and which would entail a similar outlay at no distant date for further accommodation lower down the river. They also stated they were of opinion that two crossings are immediately required, and should be sanctioned by Parliament. The one a low-level bridge at the site of the rejected duplex bridge, with two openings each about 100ft., to be spanned by a pivot bridge, the other a subway lower down the river, at or near Shadwell. Regarding the bridge, they thought the approach on the north side could be made of sufficient width by a very slight concession on the part of the War-office, and thus the heavy expenditure of purchasing any portion of the costly warehouses of the St. Katherine Dock Company could be avoided, without unduly intrenching on the precincts of the Tower, while upon the south side there appeared to be no property of very great value in the line of the proposed bridge.

The question of a swing bridge on the pivot principle of two openings, each about 100ft., they thought had been satisfactorily solved at Newcastle, where such a bridge has been constructed over the river Tyne, and has been proved capable of accommodating in a satisfactory manner both the shipping and the road traffic. They therefore unhesitatingly recommended this method of crossing the river at this site, as being most effective for relieving the congested condition of London Bridge, and affording the most direct communication between the railway depôts and warehouses on the north and the manufacturing and commercial districts on the south, and it was their opinion that this arterial communication should be constructed by one of the two great public bodies of London, either the Corporation or the Metropolitan Board of Works, and not a private company.

The result of this report was that in the following year the Corporation introduced a Bill for a low-level bridge, the main features of which were similar to those indicated by the Committee, and after an inquiry lasting nineteen days, during which time a large amount of evidence was taken, not only as to the river traffic, but as to the absolute necessity for further accommodation across the river, the Bill was passed.

The opening portion of this bridge is the feature that governs the whole design. In nearly all opening bridges in this country the movable portions swing horizontally, but in this instance a departure has been made from the general rule, and the bascule principle has been adopted; in other words, the moving parts of the bridge are made to swing in a vertical instead of a horizontal plane. A

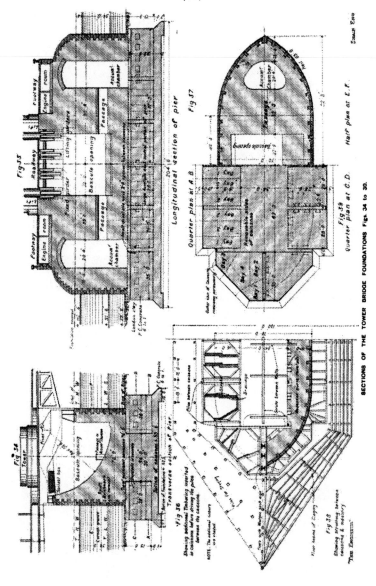

SECTIONS OF THE TOWER BRIDGE FOUNDATIONS Figs. 34 to 39.

(41)

Fig. 32—GENERAL VIEW OF MASONRY OF LOWER PARTS OF THE RIVER PIERS

bridge formed by one flap of framed timber, used to cross the moat or ditch of a fortress or castle, and capable of being drawn up by chains from the inside, so as to render the ditch impassable and block the gate or entrance, is the most ancient of all movable bridges.

When this class of structure came to be used for crossing navigable rivers and canals, these bridges were often made with two flaps, butting against each other when down, and capable of being raised by chains from posts, or by the Dutch method of overhead beams. The most important bascule bridge in this country was the one which carried the North-Eastern Railway over the river Ouse at Selby. This bridge, which has recently been replaced by a swing bridge, had a clear span of 45ft., was built in 1839, and had always worked satisfactorily. Only one man was required to open each leaf, an operation which occupies about 1¼ minutes, and had on the average to be performed eight times in twenty-four hours. One of the largest and most recent bascule bridge is that erected at Copenhagen in 1869, referred to hereafter in connection with some interest-

should consist of two side spans of 190ft. each and a centre opening span of 300ft. clear. The roadway of the side spans he proposed to carry by two wrought iron lattice girders of ordinary type, or by shallow lattice girders supported by suspension chains.

The centre span would be bridged by two hinged platforms constructed of steel for lightness. Each of these platforms would be suspended by eight pitched chains passing over polygonal barrels, fixed in the machinery placed on the piers. Balance weights would be attached to the ends of the chains within the towers. The hoisting machinery could be worked by steam power, or by hydraulic apparatus supplied by tanks fixed in the roofs over the towers. The arches between the towers carrying the polygonal chain barrels would be formed of four wrought iron braced semicircular arched ribs, connected together transversely by four wrought iron lattice frames. The rise of each arch in the centre, he suggested, should be 130ft. above high-water mark, and afford at least 100ft. clear headway for a width of 150ft. Mr.

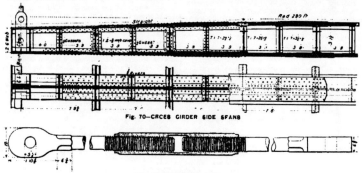

Fig. 70—CROSS GIRDER SIDE SPANS

Fig. 67—SUSPENSION RODS

ing evidence given in support of the Tower Bridge Bill when before Parliament.

There are many other examples of this class of bridge for small spans to be found at Hull, Rotterdam, and other maritime towns. The advantage derived from adopting this principle is that the long piers, required to protect the swinging portion of an ordinary bridge when it is opened, are not needed when the moving portions of such a bridge swing vertically.

This method of bridging the Thames at the Tower was suggested to a special Bridge or Subway Committee by the late City Architect, Mr. Horace Jones, during October, 1878, when he was requested to report on the various projects of Sir Joseph Bazalgette, and also to give his own views regarding the kind of bridge that he considered most suitable. Mr. Jones stated in his report that a high-level bridge, in his opinion, would not give general satisfaction, and recommended that a bridge opening on the bascule principle should be built, the leading features of which should be as follows—see Fig. 9 —the bridge when closed should allow the same headway above high water as London Bridge, namely, 29ft., and

Jones estimated the cost of such a bridge to be three-quarters of a million.

On October 31st, 1878, the Special Bridge or Subway Committee reported to the Court of Common Council that this design commended itself to them as one providing a bridge which would interfere but very slightly with the river traffic, and would bring about that relief to the commerce and trade of the city which was desired, and they therefore recommended the same for adoption, and that the necessary steps should be taken to obtain the authority of Parliament to raise the needed capital on the credit of the Bridge House Estates. This, then, was the original design for the bridge which has just been completed. On comparing it with the structure which has now been completed—Fig. 11—it will be seen that so many modifications have been made, that practically only the principle of Mr. Jones' early design has been retained. Before the Corporation applied to Parliament to grant powers to construct a bridge over the river at the Tower a deputation of the Bridge House Estates' Committee, accompanied by Mr. F. T. Reade, A.M.I.C.E., visited in the autumn of 1884 a large number of the more important opening bridges in this country as well as on the Continent, and afterwards reported on the various structures they had inspected. The following short description of the bridges examined illustrates how the problem of dealing with both road and river traffic has been solved in this country and elsewhere.

OTHER OPENING BRIDGES.

BASCULE BRIDGES.

Jan Kulten Bridge, Rotterdam.—This is a bascule bridge with two leaves of equal length, carrying a double-line tramway as well as ordinary carriage traffic over a canal 45ft. wide. This bridge, which has a clear width of 18ft., differs from the old type of bascules by having heavy back balance weights attached to the shore ends of each of the moving leaves. The time required to open or shut the bridge is from fifteen to twenty seconds, hydraulic power being used for the purpose.

Entrepôt Bridge near Rotterdam.—This is the largest bascule bridge yet constructed. It carries a single line of rails and general carriage traffic over a dock passage 72ft. in width. The bridge is 84ft. wide, and is opened and closed by hydraulic power in two to three minutes. Owing to the severe frosts in winter, glycerine has to be largely used to prevent the water actuating the machinery from freezing.

SWING BRIDGES.

Bridge at Boom, near Antwerp.—This bridge has two fixed spans of 150ft. each, one fixed span of 80ft. and a swinging portion 186ft. long revolving on a centre pier 25ft. in diameter, thus allowing two clear openings of about 80ft. each. The bridge is opened and closed by manual labour, five men being required for the purpose. The time taken for the complete operation of opening and shutting is about ten minutes.

Bridge at Koningshaven, near Rotterdam.—This bridge carries ordinary road traffic across the Koningshaven, which at this point is about 450ft. wide. There are two swing spans, one of 170ft. and one of 200ft., and each can be opened and shut by four men in one and a-half minutes. This bridge has to be opened on the average six times per hour.

Bridge over the River Tyne at Newcastle.—This bridge, which was built in 1876, has two fixed spans, one of 92½ft. and one of 64½ft., and a central swing portion 280ft. long. The width of the central pier and fenders is 60ft., so that the two clear openings are each about 110ft. The bridge, which is 50ft. wide, is worked entirely by hydraulic power, the pressure being produced by small steam engines pumping into an accumulator placed on the central pier. The accumulator has a stroke of 17ft., a ram 20in. in diameter, and is loaded to give a pressure of 700 lb. per square inch. Three hydraulic cylinders 4½in. in diameter are used for driving a horizontal shaft, with multiplying gear and pinion, working in a circular rack fixed below the centre framing.

There are two sets of machinery provided in case of a breakdown, but one set will open the bridge in one and a-half minutes. The steam engine and boiler are also in duplicate. The total weight of the swinging portion is 1450 tons, about 900 of which is supported on a central ram, the remainder resting on a train of large rollers. At each end of the bridge there are two hydraulic rams 22in.

in diameter, which are capable of slightly raising the bridge at these points to allow the bearing blocks being adjusted.

All the machinery for working the bridge is controlled by one man placed in a cabin over the central pier. The opening portion can be completely revolved in two and a-half minutes, and can be opened for a vessel to pass and closed again in three minutes.

Swing bridge at Leith Docks, Edinburgh.—This bridge, which carries two lines of rails, has a total length of 214ft. and a width of 39ft. The tail end of the bridge is 67ft. long, the clear span of the dock passage being 120ft. The total weight of the structure including the counterbalance is 620 tons, and when the bridge is swinging this is entirely supported by a central ram. When the bridge is to be opened water is admitted to this ram, which lifts 8in., raising the end of the long arm 7in., and allowing the tail end of the bridge to drop slightly and rest on a couple of rollers 80in. in diameter.

The swinging apparatus consists of a pair of hydraulic rams 14in. diameter and 10½ft. stroke, the slewing chain passing round a wrought iron ring 25ft. in diameter, fixed to the underside of the structure. The bridge can be opened in one and a-half minutes, and a vessel can pass through the dock passage and the bridge closed again in three and one-half minutes. The bridge is opened and shut about twelve times every week-day.

In the autumn of 1884, after the rejection by Parliament of Sir Joseph Bazalgette's subway and of the duplex bridge, the Corporation decided to apply at once for power to construct an opening bridge, and Mr. John Wolfe Barry was appointed engineer to the undertaking, to act in conjunction with Mr. Horace Jones, who was appointed to undertake the architectural duties connected with the structure. The original design of Mr. Jones was then reconsidered, and Mr. Barry and Mr. Jones produced a joint design—shown in Fig. 10—which provided an opening span of a clear width of 200ft., and a clear height of 135ft. above Trinity high-water mark, in lieu of the arched form of construction, as shown in Fig. 9.

The Act of Parliament was passed in the autumn of 1885, and in the summer of 1886 a contract for the foundations of the piers and abutments up to the level of 4ft. above Trinity high-water mark was let. In view of various important modifications introduced into the scheme during the passage of the Act through Parliament, the features of the superstructure required very large modifications, and the engineer and architect had commenced their investigations and studies necessary for this purpose, when the serious illness and death of Sir Horace Jones, who had received the honour of knighthood in 1885, put an end to his connection with the undertaking. Since the death of Sir Horace Jones the whole of the architectural duties, as well as those of engineering, have rested on Mr. Barry, and the design of the present bridge, as shown in Fig. 11, is the result of that reconsideration of the Parliamentary design which had just been commenced when Sir Horace Jones was taken ill.

It will be seen that the present design differs in several important particulars, both of an engineering and architectural character, from the joint design laid before Parliament. Though Mr. Barry has aimed at preserving the general appearance of the structure, he adopted a

Fig. 41—MARCH, 1892

Fig. 43—JUNE, 1892

(From photographs by Mr. W. Edward Wright and by Messrs. Perkins, Son, and Venimore)

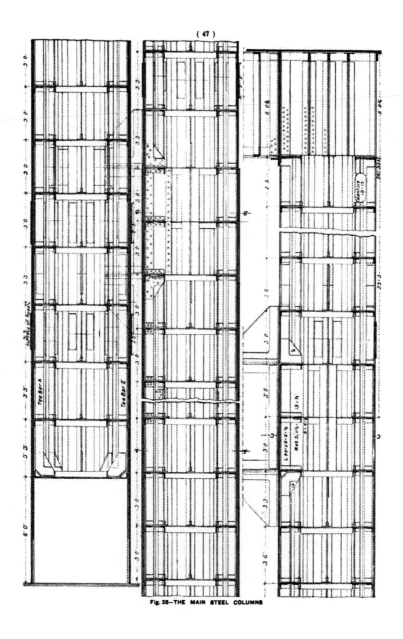

Fig. 26—THE MAIN STEEL COLUMNS

Fig. 42—APRIL, 1892

Fig. 44—OCTOBER, 1892
(From photographs by Mr. W. Edward Wright and by Messrs. Perkins, Son, and Fenimore.)

D

somewhat severer form of architecture for the main towers, while the chains, braced, and raised at the abutments, and the abutment towers themselves, are altogether new features. In the details of the architecture Mr. Barry has had the assistance of Mr. G. D. Stephenson, who was for many years one of Sir Horace Jones' staff.

In his evidence before the Parliamentary Committee Mr. Barry stated that from his observations, which had extended over five weeks, it appeared that the bridge on the average would have to be opened about twenty-two times a day, to allow such vessels through as could not pass under it, and that the operation of passing a ship through would take about five minutes; and even in the worst case observed, when several vessels followed each other, the stoppage of the road traffic would have been but twenty minutes. He estimated the bridge would take four years to build, and that its cost would be :—The bridge itself, £544,850 ; the northern approach, £19,250; southern approach, £20,900 ; which, with 10 per cent. for contingencies added, would be £585,000. To this sum must be added £165,000, the value of the land required, and this brings the total cost to £750,000. The annual expense of working was assumed to be between £3000 and £4000. With regard to the effect of the structure upon the waterway, he said that at the level of Trinity high-water the gross sectional area of the river at the site of the bridge was 24,566 square feet, which is reduced by the room taken up by the vessels moored at the tiers to 21,500 square feet. When the bridge is built these tiers are to be removed; but the space occupied by the new piers will reduce the gross sectional area above mentioned to 20,000 square feet, consequently the net reduction will be some 7 per cent. In the case of London Bridge, he stated that the corresponding areas are :—Gross area, 19,962 square feet; net area, after deducting space occupied by the bridge piers and the steamboat pier, 16,802 square feet; showing a reduction in the gross area of about 16 per cent.

Mr. W. F. Luders, Captain of the Port of Copenhagen, gave some interesting evidence relating to the seven bascule bridges under his charge in that city. The most important of these is the one completed in 1869, and shown by Fig. 13. The span of this bridge is 60ft., and the two moving leaves are worked by hydraulic power ; although hand gearing and machinery actuated by compressed air is also provided for use during the winter. When hydraulic power is used, the time taken to open and close the bridge is about one minute; but this operation, when done by hand power, takes about half as long again. The average number of vessels passing through this bridge per diem is twenty, although as many as fifty-five have passed in one day; and in such a case the aggregate stoppage of the road traffic was about three and a-half hours. The maximum daily traffic over the bridge is about 500 vehicles and 3500 passengers. This witness had not observed any difficulties arising from the velocity of the current through the bridge, which sometimes was as high as three and a-half miles per hour. The area of each leaf is 1000 square feet, and the top of the leaf when the bridge is open is about 40ft. above the level of the water. The annual cost of working the bridge varied from £370 to £440.

When the Tower Bridge Bill came before the House of Lords, the contention of the opponents was as to whether the wharfingers were entitled to compensation for depreciation of property, and the Committee decided that the Corporation should in some way provide against the contingencies of injury to business, and a clause was inserted in the Bill, after a prolonged discussion, to the following effect:—If, at the expiration of four years after the opening of the Tower Bridge for traffic, the owner, lessee, or occupier of any of the wharves or quays between the bridge and London Bridge shall allege that such premises are depreciated in value by reason of danger or delay caused by the bridge to vessels destined for such premises, and shall give the necessary notices, and claim compensation, then, if an agreement be not come to with the Corporation for the settlement of such claim, it shall be referred to arbitration to decide whether there has been depreciation, and the amount payable, if that should be found to be sustained. The aggregate amount of compensation in respect of all interests in any such premises shall not exceed two years' purchase of the assessable value in force on the 1st of January, 1886; and such aggregate amount shall be in full satisfaction of all compensation payable to all parties interested in such premises. No claim shall be sustainable unless made within seven years of the opening of the bridge for traffic. No compensation shall be given for any danger or delay caused during the construction of the bridge to vessels destined for such premises. No compensation shall be awarded for any quay or wharf on the south side of the Thames south of a line 200ft. back from the river front or its quay. In respect to a petition of the ferrymen plying between the stairs near the bridge, it was decided that the Corporation shall pay compensation for damage done through interference with their rights; such compensation to be settled by agreement or by arbitration. As no compensation could be obtained until four years had elapsed after the opening of the bridge for traffic, it was stated that the resources of the Bridge House Estates would be able to meet any such demands as were substantiated, and the Committee, regarding the great need which existed for the bridge, recommended that the clauses should be accepted, and the Bill proceeded with.

The Act received the Royal Assent on August 14th, 1885, and on the 21st of June, 1886, the Prince of Wales, on behalf of her Majesty the Queen, laid the foundation stone for the new bridge. In 1889 it was found necessary to apply to Parliament for an extension of time for the completion of the work, as only four years were allowed by the Act for the construction of the bridge, and such extension was granted to August 14th, 1893. In the early part of 1893, owing to the many unforeseen difficulties that had arisen, it was evident that a still further extension of time would be needed, and Parliament was again applied to, and granted an additional year's extension to complete the work.

The Tower Bridge is, in appearance, unlike any structure that has yet been built. The originality exhibited in the design is shown particularly in combining heavy steelwork with masonry of elaborate architectural character, the provision of high-level footways for use when the central portion of the bridge is open for the river traffic, and the application of the bascule principle on a scale never before attempted.

The staging used during the construction of the work has not at present been wholly removed, and consequently prevents to a large extent a correct impression being formed of the general appearance of the structure. The durable character of the large river piers is one of the features of the work, and had Macaulay foreseen what a substantial structure was to be built in the vicinity of St. Paul's, he would have no doubt considered it better suited to the physical requirements of his artistic New Zealander than the broken arch of London Bridge.

GENERAL DESCRIPTION OF THE FINAL DESIGN.

On referring to the map of the site—Fig. 18, page 31, and Plate I.—it will be seen that the entrance to the bridge on the north side of the river is situated almost immediately opposite to the Mint.

From this point the approach passes along the east side of the Tower of London to the shore, where the northern abutment is placed on the west side of the wharf belonging to the General Steam Navigation Company. The approach, which is formed of a series of brick arches generally 15ft. span, rises from the level of the ground at its commencement by the easy gradient of 1 in 60. It is nearly 1000ft. long, and turns slightly to the west just before it reaches the river. The roadway is 35ft. wide, and on either side of it is a footway 12½ft. wide.

The south abutment is placed a little to the westward of Horselydown stairs, and the approach on this side of the river is about 800ft. long, and runs in a straight line from this point, on a falling gradient of 1 in 40, until it meets Tooley-street. This approach is similar to the one on the north side of the river, the roadway being 35ft. wide and each of the footways 12½ft. wide. Stairs are provided at both abutments for people to ascend from the banks of the river to the roadway of the bridge. The width of the river between the faces of the north and south abutments is 880ft., and this distance is divided into two side spans, each having a clear opening of 270ft., and one central span of 200ft. clear, making together 740ft., the difference between this and the total length to be bridged over is occupied by the two river piers, each of which is 70ft. wide. The maximum range of the tide is 25ft., and is from 8½ft. above Trinity high-water mark to 21½ft. below it. The ordinary springs range 21ft., and neaps 17ft. The depth of the water in the opening span is 38½ft. at high-water.

The clear headway allowed above Trinity high-water is 28ft. and 20ft. at the north and south abutments respectively, and 27ft. on the shore side, of each of the piers. At each end of the middle span there is only 15ft. headway; but in the centre there is 29½ft. from high-water to the under side of the structure when the bridge is closed, and when the moving leaves are open for the river traffic the clear headway is about 143ft.

The roadway along each of the side spans is 35ft. wide, with a 12½ft. footway on each side; but over the central span the width of the road is reduced to 32ft., and each of the footways to 8½ft. The gradient of the side spans is 1 in 67½ and 1 in 38½ for the north and south sides of the river respectively, but over the central span it is 1 in 89½. The north and south river piers—Fig. 32, page 41—are similar in all respects, and are, we believe, the largest of their kind in the world, the area of the two piers at the level of the foundations being about equal to the whole of the twelve circular piers carrying the Forth Bridge.

The only other foundations of such dimensions are those of the Brooklyn Bridge, the two main piers of which support a roadway of 1606ft. span.

The large size of the Tower Bridge piers is due to the pressure upon the London clay on which they rest being limited to four tons per square foot, and to the great weight of the towers, and the high and low-level roadways which they support. The maximum load that can come on the foundations is very nearly 70,000 tons, and with the above pressure per square foot each pier requires to be about 205ft. by 100ft. to give the necessary area. It might be at first considered that four tons per square foot is a rather small pressure to allow on such a material as London clay, but when it is remembered how serious any appreciable settlement of the piers might be to the complicated machinery, and the masonry superstructure placed upon them, it will be generally admitted that it was wise not to exceed this moderate load. The settlement of the piers under the total dead load was estimated to be 3in.; observations already taken, however, show that it will be somewhat less than this amount. Before the size of the piers was determined, experiments were made on a cylinder 6ft. in diameter, sunk into the ground at the site of the bridge, and loaded so that a pressure of four tons per square foot was obtained; the settlement at the end of two days was in this case 1½in. After the loading on this cylinder was increased so that the pressure on the clay was six and a-half tons per square foot, the settlement kept on increasing.

In Charing Cross railway bridge, which is carried by cast iron cylinders 14ft. in diameter, filled with concrete and brickwork, and sunk from 20ft. to 50ft. below the bed of the river, the maximum pressure would be eight tons per square foot if the bridge were loaded with locomotives, although this pressure might be reduced by one ton per square foot if the friction between the cylinders and the ground could be relied on. Each cylinder when completed up to the level of high-water mark was tested by placing upon it 450 tons of rails. This loading, added to the weight of the cylinder, caused a pressure of six tons per square foot on the London clay, and the permanent settlement averaged 3in. On two of the cylinders the loading was increased to 700 tons, causing the total pressure upon the clay to be nearly eight tons per square foot. The permanent settlement in both these cases was 4in.

In other Thames bridges, such as that carrying the London, Brighton, and South Coast Railway at Victoria, the load on the foundations does not exceed five tons per square foot, and in the new bridge of the London, Chatham, and Dover Railway at Blackfriars, it is four and three-quarter tons per square foot when the bridge is fully loaded.

The piers were sunk by caissons, open at the top, to a depth of about 19ft. below the bed of the river, but the foundations were carried down 7ft. further, and the sides of the caissons were undercut 5ft. beyond the cutting edge. The portion of the piers below the river bed is composed of concrete, while the upper part is formed of gault brickwork in cement, faced with Cornish granite.

The roadway of the bridge is entirely supported by the steelwork of the superstructure—as shown in Figs. 19 et seq., Plate III.—which does the whole of the useful work, although for architectural reasons it is hidden from view by the masonry which envelopes it. On each of

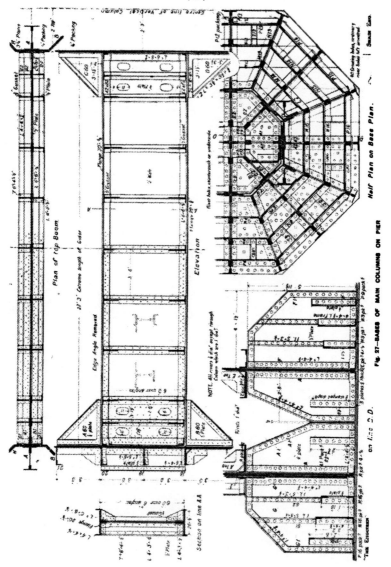

Fig. 27—BASES OF MAIN COLUMNS ON PIER

the piers, resting on massive granite bedstones, are four octagonal columns, built up of flat steel plates, connected together at their edges by splayed angle-bars. These are 120ft. high, and 5½ft. in diameter, and are all securely braced together. At the height of about 60ft. above the surface of the roadway these columns are connected together by plate girders 6ft. deep, between which smaller girders are placed, forming a floor, or, as it is termed, the first landing. Another similar landing occurs about 28ft. higher, and the tops of all columns are joined to each other by girders of a similar character, although somewhat heavier. Between these horizontal girders diagonal bracing, consisting of flat steel plates, is adopted, except where such would interfere with the clear space required for the roadway, and in such cases curved struts are substituted—Fig. 23, Plate III.

At the height of about 148ft. above Trinity high water there are two footways, carried by girders, supported on the top of the columns on each pier. Each of these footways is 12ft. wide, and some 280ft. long, and is intended to be used by foot-passengers when prevented crossing the river, owing to the moving portion of the bridge being opened to allow vessels to pass up or down the stream. Two hydraulic lifts are placed on each pier to convey people from the lower to the higher level and vice versâ; stairs are also provided for any who prefer walking to using the lifts. At a height of 28ft. above the top of the columns there is another landing, carrying the steel principals and rafters which support the roof.

Four similar octagonal columns rest upon both the north and south abutments; they are, however, smaller, being only some 44ft. high, and 4½'t. diameter. These are built up of flat steel plates, in the same manner as the pier columns, and are braced together by horizontal and inclined plate girders on the east and west sides of the bridge, but on the north and south faces these columns are connected by plate girders, the under side of which is in the form of an arch. About five miles of steel plates were required to form the columns on the piers and abutments.

The side spans, each of which is 270ft. clear, are supported by chains, and are really suspension bridges. The chains consist of two links only, joined together at their lowest point by a pin 2½ft. in diameter, their upper ends being carried by the columns on the piers and abutments. The horizontal component of the weight is conveyed over the abutment columns by steel links which are connected to inclined ties, the lower ends of which are securely anchored to massive concrete foundations.

The horizontal pull from the chains resting on the south pier columns is nearly balanced by that exerted from those which rest on the north pier, their ends being connected across the river by flat ties 301ft. long, each composed of eight plates 2ft. wide and 1in. thick, carried by the outside girders of the high-level footways.

These chains would, of course, only balance each other when the weight on both sides of the river was the same. To provide, however, for the effect of unequal loading, and extremes of temperature, the lower pins which connect the chains of the south span together are fixed to the masonry abutment by what have been called the "stiffening" girders.

The floor of these side spans is formed of cross girders, each about 61ft. long and 2½ft. deep. These are placed 18ft. apart, and are suspended to the chains by rods from 5½in. to 6in. diameter. Between these cross girders longitudinal floor girders are placed 7½ft. apart, and these carry a floor composed of corrugated steel-plates. A massive cast iron parapet is fixed along each side of these spans.

The general arrangement of the opening portion of the bridge is represented in Fig. 20, which shows a vertical section through the centre line of either pier. Two girders are fixed on the north and south sides of each pier, J and H, each 52ft. long, and these support the ends of the eight "fixed" girders F, which are placed parallel to the centre line of the bridge. These girders carry the large pedestals forming the bearings for the main pivot shaft A, which is 48ft. long and 1ft. 9in. diameter.

The opening portion, or leaf, as it is generally called, consists of four girders B, 18½ft. apart, all of which are rigidly braced together. At the shore end of each leaf a ballast chamber is filled with some 290 tons of lead and about 60 tons of cast iron, for the purpose of balancing the portion of the leaf projecting over the pier. The small space that was available for the counterbalance, and the short leverage which could be given it, made it desirable, and even economical, to use this considerable quantity of lead besides cast iron. The position of the counterweight is such that the pivot shaft passes through the centre of gravity of the whole leaf, which is therefore perfectly balanced in all positions.

The total weight of each leaf is very nearly 1200 tons, and although this is a considerable mass to set in motion, yet, being balanced on and fixed to a shaft resting on live rollers, the theoretical power required to open the bridge is not great.

A quadrant—C—is attached to each of the lower portions of the outside girders forming the leaf, and to its circumference cast steel teeth are fixed. The leaf is caused to rotate about the main pivot shaft A by means of the pinions D, which are geared into the teeth on the quadrants.

The hydraulic pressure which is used for opening the bridge, and for other purposes, is generated near the accumulator house, built on the east side of the southern approach, as shown hereafter. The machinery consists of two steam pumping engines, each of 360-horse power, eight large hydraulic engines, and six accumulators, the pressure being conveyed to the piers through cast iron pipes, laid along the southern shore span to the hydraulic engines on the south pier, and continued up the inside of one of the steel columns on this pier, along the top of the east high-level footway, and down one of the columns on the north pier to the hydraulic engines for opening the northern leaf. The boilers and pumps for supplying the pressure occupy four of the arches forming the south approach.

It was the general opinion of Parliament and the Corporation that the bridge at the Tower should be treated not merely as an engineering structure, but that it should possess an architectural character which would be in accordance with that of the Tower of London itself, and not mar the striking group which that venerable structure affords. In fact, at one time it was stipulated by the Tower authorities that a castellated fortification at the north abutment should form part of the undertaking. When also it was seen that the quadrants which actuate the moving leaves, and which project some 40ft. above the roadway, had to be inclosed from the weather and protected from risk of injury, and when it was desired that there should be spacious stairs and lifts for pedestrians in the towers, it was apparent that (1) the towers could not be of the solid masonry which would have been necessary to carry by itself the weight of the upper and lower bridges, and (2) that some large amount of the columns and connecting girders which are necessary to support the chains and upper bridge must be in some way inclosed. If masonry, therefore, had not been for other reasons desirable, some other material, such as cast iron, must have been employed; and after study of the subject, when designs for an iron or steel superstructure were well considered, it was decided to adhere to the masonry as an architectural feature, and the more so from the near propinquity of the Tower of London. The masonry has, as far as possible, been designed to follow the main features of the steel columns and connecting girders, as will be observed when one traces the form of the granite columns at the angles of the towers, and the horizontal bands which follow the lines of the connecting girders.

It has been argued that the manner in which the steelwork has been concealed by the masonry superstructure is similar to the way in which the skeleton of the human body is enveloped and hidden by the flesh, but on examination it will be found that these are not really parallel cases.

From an engineering point of view objections might be raised to this method of construction, which at first sight may be thought to be of far greater consequence than any æsthetical considerations. These are the effect of expansion and contraction of the steelwork, and the question of the difficulty of preventing corrosion of the metal framework where it is enveloped in masonry and cannot be painted. With regard to the effect on the masonry, caused by any alteration of temperature or compression of the steelwork, there is, in this instance, little cause for anxiety. The largest buildings are now very often supported on a framework of metal columns and girders, without any special provision being made for the effect of changes of temperature, and the many high buildings carried by girders over the underground railway in London show that its influence may in such cases be entirely ignored. In such buildings as the Crystal Palace, and the large roof at the St. Pancras Station, no special arrangements appear needed to provide for expansion and contraction of the ironwork.

In order to prevent any adhesion between the masonry and the steelwork at the Tower Bridge, the columns were covered with canvas as the masonry was built around them, and spaces were left in such places where any subsequent compression of the steelwork would bring undue weight upon the adjacent stonework. The envelope of masonry acts as a most potent protection against extremes of temperature, and so far as present experience at the bridge goes, where already we have had very high and very low thermometers, no effect whatever has been discerned affecting the concord between the steel and the masonry.

Again, with respect to protection from corrosion, it is considered by Mr. Barry, as the result of much experience, that no mode exists which so effectually stops corrosion of iron or steel as a protection of brickwork, masonry, or concrete, and for many years past in railway and other structures it has been his practice, and that

of other engineers, to envelope as much as possible of girders in such materials. Where, in re-construction of work, it has been necessary to pull down ironwork embedded in brickwork or concrete, it has been universally found that the iron has been free from corrosion, and is in the same condition as when first built in.

In this bridge, therefore, all parts of the metal to which access for painting purposes cannot be afterwards obtained have been thoroughly coated with Portland cement. Manholes have been provided in all the steel columns, the interior of which can therefore be painted whenever necessary. The bearings for the chains over the columns, the large pins, and the stiffening girders for the Surrey span, show perhaps more than any other portion of the structure the large amount of time and originality that has been bestowed upon every part of the bridge, many portions of which demanded special and novel treatment.

The following dimensions and approximate quantities of materials will give a general idea of the magnitude of the undertaking:—The total length of the bridge, including both approaches, is just half a mile. The total height of the towers on the piers, measured from the level of the foundations, is 298ft., so that if these piers were imagined to be resting on the ground by the side of St. Paul's Cathedral, they would appear as indicated in the sketch page 68.

For the construction of this bridge some 285,000 cubic feet of granite and other stone, 20,000 tons of cement, 70,000 cubic yards of concrete, 31,000,000 bricks, and 14,000 tons of iron and steel have been used.

The somewhat unusual course of dividing the work between different contractors led to no less than eight contracts being made in connection with the bridge. Several of the different portions of the work were of course being carried out at the same time. The name of the contractor to whom each was entrusted is given in the following table:—

Table showing the Contractors for various portions of the Tower Bridge.

No. of contract	Date of commencement	Description of work.	Name of contractor.
1	Mar., 1886	The piers and abutments	Mr. John Jackson
2	Feb., 1887	The northern approach, including north anchorage girder.	Do.
3	Dec., 1887	Cast iron parapet for northern approach.	Do.
4	July, 1888	Southern approach, including south anchorage girder.	Mr. Wm. Webster
5	Dec., 1887	Hydraulic machinery	Sir W. G. Armstrong, Mitchell, & Co., Ld.
6	May, 1889	Iron and steel superstructure.	Sir Wm. Arrol & Co., Ld.
7	May, 1883	Masonry superstructure	Messrs. Perry & Co.
8	May, 1892	Paving and lighting	Do.

Contract No. 1 was for the two river piers and the two abutments, up to the level of 4ft. above Trinity high-water mark. Contract No. 7 was for all the masonry on the piers and the two abutments, above the level of 4ft. above Trinity high-water mark.

Fig. 73—THE MIDDLESEX MAIN PIER AND HIGH LEVEL FOOTWAYS—VIEW FROM SOUTH
(From Photograph by Mr. W. E. Wright)

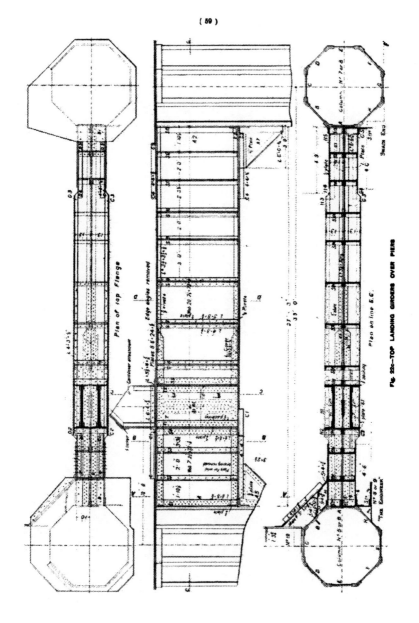

Fig. 22.—TOP LANDING GIRDERS OVER PIERS

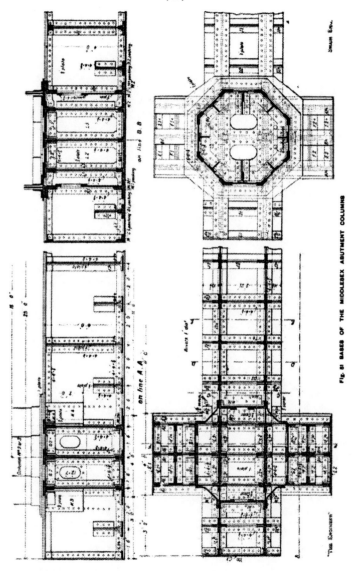

Fig. 61 BASES OF THE MIDDLESEX ABUTMENT COLUMNS

THE FOUNDATIONS.

In the early part of last year, Mr. G. E. W. Cruttwell, M.I.C.E., who has acted as Resident Engineer throughout the construction of the Tower Bridge, read a paper on the "Pier Foundations" before the Institution of Civil Engineers, and the following account of this portion of the work has been obtained almost entirely from that source, the writer of the present description not being at that time engaged upon the bridge.

In laying the foundations for the two river piers it was necessary to use caissons of some kind, as timber coffer-dams were prohibited for the purpose by the Act of Parliament. The caissons used are 90ft. by 194½ft., but the foundations are 100ft. by 204½ft., as the London clay upon which the piers rest rendered it possible to effect a considerable saving in the cost, by contracting the limits of the caissons within the outside line of the foundations, and undercutting beneath them about 5ft. horizontally to obtain the required area.

A clause in the Tower Bridge Act rendered it compulsory to always maintain a clear waterway of 160ft. between the piers while the bridge was being constructed. Consequently the two piers could not be built at the same time, as the staging necessary would have occupied far too much of the river space, but by adopting a system of small caissons round the circumference of the piers instead of one large caisson extending right across a pier, it was possible while building one of the piers to be also working at the shore side of the other. Had both piers proceeded simultaneously a saving of thirteen to fourteen months might have been effected. As it was, however, the excavation of one side of one pier had to be deferred until the staging could be cleared away from the neighbouring side of the other pier. On the north and south faces of each pier there is a row of four caissons, each 28ft. square, joined at each end by a pair of triangular-shaped caissons, formed approximately to the shape of the cutwaters—Fig. 39. There is a space of 2½ft. between all the caissons, this being considered the least dimension in which workmen could be effectively employed. The caissons enclose a rectangular space 34ft. by 124½ft., which was not excavated until the permanent work forming the outside portion of the pier had been built, both in the caissons and between them, up to a height of 4ft. above Trinity high-water mark.

The extreme limits of the necessary staging round the piers—Fig.38—were restricted to a breadth of 130ft. and a length of 335ft., so as to avoid obstructing the waterway of the Thames more than was absolutely necessary, but this area of staging, although extensive, was found insufficient for carrying out the work expeditiously. There were two rows of piles surrounding each pier, about 18½ft. apart, the inner row being driven some 6ft. from the caissons, so that it might be clear of the toe of the undercut portion of the foundations. The piles were spaced about 15ft. apart, and driven from 15ft. to 20ft. beneath the bed of the river, and were connected together both longitudinally and transversely by walings and other timber bracing. Within the portion of the pier enclosed by the caissons the staging was formed of three rows of piles spaced the same distance apart as those above referred to.

Sketch Showing Relative Heights of Tower Bridge and St. Paul's

In September, 1886, the erection of the first caisson was commenced. Timbers were placed between the central and outer stages, a little above low water, to form a low-level platform for the caisson to be built upon, vertically over the position it was ultimately to occupy—Fig. 31. All the caissons were in two portions, the permanent part being 19ft. in height, and the temporary part resting upon it being 88ft. high. Each portion consisted of a single skin of wrought iron plate, ½in. thick at the bottom of the permanent caisson, diminishing to ¼in. plates at the top of the temporary caisson. A rolled steel cutting edge was attached to the bottom of the lower caissons, being riveted on the outer side of the skin, so that it projected ¾in. beyond the side plates, thus somewhat reducing the surface friction of sinking. Every 3ft. this cutting edge was stiffened by rolled iron joists placed vertically, and supported by two horizontal frames of 15in. pine timbers, having diagonal struts at each of the four corners—see Fig. 28. These joints also served as covers to the skin plates, which were placed with their long edges vertical.

Above the joists the remainder of the permanent caisson was formed of ½in. and 7/16in. plates, 7ft. long and 3½ft. wide, placed with their long edges horizontally. The vertical joints were covered by T irons on the outside, and with flat strips on the inside, but the horizontal joints were covered only on the inside by angle irons of sufficient width to take a double line of rivets, and which also served to support the timber frames used for staging the skin above each of the horizontal joints. These frames were composed of 14in. pitch pine timbers, with diagonal struts at each of the corners.

The temporary caisson was similar to the upper portion of the permanent one, but somewhat lighter, the skin plates diminishing from ⅜in. at the bottom to ¼in. at the top. The timber frames were also reduced from 14in. square to half-timbers 12in. by 6in.

The water-tight joint between the temporary and permanent caissons was made by a small strip of india-rubber ⅜in. diameter, as shown in Fig. 80. As an additional precaution a second strip of india-rubber, ⅜in. in diameter, was laid outside the skin plates between two angle irons, but the joints proved so water-tight, that after the first five caissons had been sunk, this extra strip was omitted in the remaining cases.

As the Tower Bridge Act provided that the piers should not exceed 70ft. in width within a depth of 84ft. below Trinity high-water mark, the highest level for the joint between the temporary and permanent caisson was necessarily fixed.

For facility of erection and removal, the temporary caisson was divided horizontally into four sections. As previously mentioned, all the caissons were sunk so that there was a space of 2¼ft. between each adjoining pair. For the purpose of connecting them together after sinking, two angle irons were riveted on at each corner—see Fig. 29—so as to form grooves extending from the top of the temporary to the bottom of the permanent caisson. After the caissons had been sunk, piles were driven between them within these grooves, thus closing these narrow spaces. The first pile was fitted with a sheeting shoe, so that in driving it was kept hard against the pile groove, the closing pile being diamond-pointed. Vertical joints were made in the skin plates of the temporary caissons, close to these pile grooves, so that the sides of the caissons could be easily removed after the piles were driven.

The permanent caissons were made by Messrs. Head, Wrightson, and Co., and were delivered at the site in four pieces. These were lowered upon the platform, situated a little above low water, where the complete caisson was built and riveted. When the ironwork was together the timber frames were fixed in place, and all was then ready to lower the caisson to the bed of the river. To accomplish this two pairs of trussed timber beams were placed above the caisson, their ends resting upon the staging as shown in Fig. 81. Four lowering rods with screwed ends were connected to the corner rolled iron joists, and the caisson was first raised sufficiently to allow of the stage, upon which it had been built, being cleared away, and then lowered gradually to the bottom of the river. The first sections of the temporary caisson were then put into position and divers sent down to level the surface of the ground, so as to secure a more uniform bearing round the cutting edge. The sinking was then commenced and additional lengths were added to the lowering rods as the caisson descended. The rods were retained in position until the undercutting beneath the cutting edge was completed, and the concrete filling was in place.

The upper sections were built on the temporary caisson as soon as the sinking had advanced far enough to allow sufficient head-room for their erection beneath the trussed beams. The temporary caissons were divided into four sections horizontally for facility of erection and removal, and were constructed by Messrs. Bow and McLachlan. The material excavated was London clay, covered in places by about a foot of ballast, and so tough that after the caissons had been sunk 4ft. or 5ft. into it, the water could be pumped out without fear of the river forcing its way beneath the cutting edge. The excavation was done by Priestman grabs for a depth of 5ft. to 6ft. beneath the bottom frames. These grabs only worked in the middle portion of the caissons, and divers were

employed to excavate the material round the sides and beneath the diagonal struts, and to shovel it towards the centre, within reach of the grabs.

The caissons were supported by the lowering rods, when the excavation was commenced, to prevent them sinking to such a depth that the divers would be unable to work under the lower frames, but when the material had been excavated from beneath, the caissons were allowed to descend gradually. As the cutting edge penetrated the surface it became necessary to permit the free rise and fall of the tide within the caissons in order to prevent any inequality of water pressure forcing a passage beneath it.

After a depth of 2ft. to 3ft. below the river bed had been attained, there was sufficient head-room under the trussed beams to allow the second section of the temporary caisson being put into place, and when this was done the timber frames immediately above low-water were loaded at the corners with kentledge.

In the case of the north pier, the weight thus added was, on the average, 75 tons for each caisson, and its effect was to force the caissons from 4ft. to 6ft. into the clay. At this depth it was considered safe to pump them dry, and trust to the clay [to resist the water pressure. The pumps were set to work a short time before half ebb, and in about two hours, by the time the tide had fallen to within 2ft. or 3ft. of low-water, or within about 25ft. of the cutting edge, all the water was pumped out. Navvies then went down and continued to work for two or three hours, filling the skips, until the rise of the tide rendered it expedient to stop, and allow the caisson to fill again by opening the sluices. As the sinking advanced, the pumping was commenced earlier, and the sluices were kept shut longer, so that when a depth of about 18ft. below the bed of the river was attained the time for excavation was about six hours every tide. In this way the caissons were sunk about 19ft. below the river bed, and at this depth it was considered that the undercutting would be a comparatively safe operation. The weight of a square caisson, including the timbering, was 166 tons, and that of an angle caisson 207 tons. The maximum weight of kentledge added was 274 tons, in the case of a square caisson at the north pier, and the minimum was 86 tons for one of the angle caissons of the south pier. For the square caissons the average weight of kentledge was 208 tons, and 181 tons for the north and south piers respectively, and 102 tons and 92 tons for the angle caissons. The rate of progress of the sinking, when it was done by the Priestman grabs and divers, and before the caissons were pumped dry, was, on the average, 8in. a day. In a square caisson, to accomplish this, there were four divers, and in an angle caisson, six divers at work for nine hours each day. When, however, it became possible to pump the caissons dry for an average of four hours at each tide the daily descent increased to 16in., and after the final exclusion of the tide, a double shift of navvies was employed, resulting in the rate of sinking being increased to 8ft. 9in. a day. There were, on the average, twenty-four men and twenty men employed in the square and angle caissons respectively.

In arriving at the above average results of the sinking the rates of two of the caissons have been omitted, because in those cases considerable delays occurred. The first was due to the removal of some moorings from

(C5)

Fig. 77—THE SURREY MAIN PIER FROM THE SOUTH
From Photographs by Mr. W. E. Wright)

E

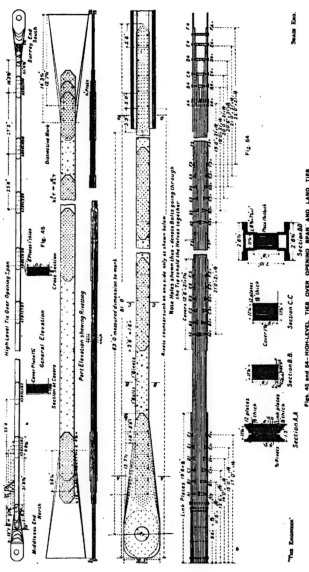

Figs. 45 and 54.—HIGH-LEVEL TIES OVER OPENING SPAN AND LAND TIES

"The Engineer"

Swan Eng.

near the site of one of the square caissons at the north pier, which had left a hole extending, it was thought, to a depth of 5ft. beneath the surface. The caisson was, therefore, sunk to a depth of 11ft. before pumping out, and, after two days of tide-work, the water was excluded. Two more days had passed, and the cutting edge had reached a depth of 16ft. beneath the river bed when a " blow " occurred, and the water rushed in through a rent in the clay, which extended to a depth of about 9in. below the cutting edge. The solid clay intervening between the rent and the ordinary level of the cutting edge, when sunk to its usual depth, amounted only to 3ft., so that this caisson was sunk somewhat deeper than the others to gain a sufficient thickness of clay to withstand the water-pressure before again pumping out. The temporary caisson was therefore made 2ft. higher by a couple of timbers bolted all round the top, and the sinking was continued by divers to a depth of 1½ft. below the ordinary level. Towards low-water the water was pumped out from the caisson, and, before the tide rose, the bottom in the neighbourhood of the blow was cleaned off, and the concrete was filled in to a height of 2ft. above the cutting edge. The sluices were then opened, and three days were allowed for the concrete to set before the water in the caisson was again pumped out. The water was now finally excluded, and the remaining operations were conducted as in the case of the other caissons.

The second blow took place in one of the angle caissons at the south pier, and was due to a stage pile in the narrow space between the two angle caissons being driven in a slanting direction so that, as the caisson went down, its cutting edge came in contact with the pile, and thus loosened the clay in the immediate neighbourhood. The blow occurred whilst the water was being pumped out for the first time, the cutting edge of the caisson at the time being 18½ft. below the river bed. This left a depth of 5½ft. to be sunk by the divers, before the caisson attained its full depth. The adjoining angle caisson had been previously sunk, and the blow being in the space between the two, all danger of another mishap was averted by driving the piles and removing the water from the narrow space between them, before again pumping.

The sides of the caissons forming the circumference of the pier were undercut 5ft. beyond the cutting edge, and 7ft. below it—see Fig. 28—and, in addition, each caisson was undercut for a width of 2½ft. below the spaces intervening between it and the adjoining caissons. When all the piles were driven between the caissons, so that they formed a continuous band round the pier, communication between the river and the water, in the central portion of the pier, was maintained by means of a 12in. pipe, consequently there was very little difference in the pressures on either side of the caissons.

As soon as a section of the undercutting was completed, concrete composed of six of Thames ballast to one of Portland cement was lowered into the caissons by skips, and the spaces filled in. No regular layers were adhered to, but as a rule the concrete was shot from the skips, and slightly spread with the shovel so as to form irregular layers about 18in. in thickness.

To effect a satisfactory junction between the concrete in the caisson and that in the central portion of the pier, dovetails were formed along the sides, as shown in Fig. 39. These dovetails extended from about 6in. above the cutting edge up to the level of the top of the

concrete, which was about 2ft. below the top of the permanent caisson. The work remained at this level until a more extensive area for building the masonry than that afforded by a single caisson could be obtained by the removal of the sides, and bonding between adjacent caissons.

The piers, from the river bed upwards, are faced with rough picked Cornish granite, in courses between 2ft. and 2½ft. in thickness. The interior work is built with wire-cut gault bricks, except where special strength is required, as in the part which supports the opening span, and the inside face work, which are of Staffordshire brindle bricks. All the work is set in Portland cement mortar, 2½ to 1 for the gault brickwork, and 1½ to 1 for the brindle brick-work and granite.

Before finally excluding the tide from the central portion of the pier, five timber struts were placed between the walls, at the level of high-water—see Fig. 38. These were required to prevent the external water pressure from unduly compressing the clay beneath the inner edge of the concrete foundations. When the water was drained away from this central portion, it was found that the north pier had silted up 14ft. above the original level of the river bed during the interval of thirteen months, and the south pier nearly 13ft. in a somewhat shorter time.

The excavation of this portion of the piers was carried down over the whole surface to a depth of some 5ft. below the tops of the permanent caissons, but below this level it was taken out in four sections, no two adjoining ones being excavated at the same time, so that the walls should never be unsupported for a greater length than 30ft. As the walls proved quite water-tight, except for a slight weeping through the concrete, no pumping was necessary during the time this excavation was in progress.

Considerable delay occurred through all vessels and barges arriving at the works being compelled by the Thames Conservators to moor on the shore side of the piers, in order that the navigation of the central water-way should not be impeded. This necessitated much additional labour in handling materials and plant required for carrying out the work.

As already mentioned, the staging that could be constructed round the piers was far too restricted for the rapid execution of the work. The plant alone occupied a large part of the stages, and deducting the space for the crane roads, little room remained for the storage of material, which had consequently to be ordered in comparatively small quantities at a time, and frequent delays resulted from the failure of their delivery at the required moment. The plant used for each pier consisted of three Priestman 5-ton travelling cranes and grabs, three Booth 4-ton travelling cranes, and one 4-ton Scotch crane. The pumps used were a 10in. Gwynne centrifugal, a 12in. Owen direct-acting force pump, and two 2in. Pulsometer pumps. The remainder of the plant consisted of boilers, engine for compressing air, diving gear, and such like necessary apparatus. The works at night were lit up by five Lucigen lamps, each of 2500-candle power, on each pier.

The total cost of the two piers, to a height of 4ft. above Trinity high-water mark, including all temporary works, amounted to £111,122. The principal items comprised in this sum are shown on page 70.

The first four items may be regarded as subsidiary to

the execution of the concrete, brickwork, and granite, which form the permanent portion of the work.

Total Cost of the Two Piers.

140,000 cubic feet of timbering in staging, caissons, &c
997 tons of wrought iron and steel in 24 permanent caissons.
915 tons of wrought iron in 18 temporary caissons.
27,710 cubic yards of excavation, exclusive of 4200 cubic yards of silt.

25,220 cubic yards	of Portland cement concrete, 6 to 1.	
20,600	,, ,,	Gault brickwork in cement.
1,800	,, ,,	Staffordshire brindle brickwork in cement.
3,340	,, ,,	Cornish granite.
50 960	,, ,,	total, concrete, brickwork, and granite.

Dividing the total cost by the cubic contents of the last-named items, the average cost works out to be £2 3s. 7d. per cubic yard. The contractor for the construction of both of these piers up to a level of 4ft. above Trinity high-water mark was Mr. John Jackson, of Westminster.

THE STEEL SUPERSTRUCTURE.

In July, 1889, the contract for the construction and erection of the steelwork for the bridge was let to Sir William Arrol and Co., of Dalmarnock Ironworks, Glasgow. This contract included the supply and erection at the site of some 11,000 tons of steel, about 1200 tons of ornamental cast ironwork, and the 580 tons of lead required for counterbalancing the moving leaves of the opening span. The steel used throughout the whole of the work was made by the Siemens-Martin process, and has a tensile strength of from 27 to 32 tons per square inch of sectional area, and an ultimate elongation of 20 per cent. in a length of 8in. Mr. C. J. Jackaman, A.M.I.C.E., represented the engineer at the contractor's works during the construction of the bridge, and also tested the whole of the materials used in this portion of the superstructure. The steel angles, tees, and plates required for the work were supplied by The Steel Company of Scotland, A. and J. Stewart and Clydesdale, and by several other leading manufacturers in the neighbourhood of Glasgow. The ornamental cast iron parapets, and the decorative panels for the high-level footways were made by Messrs. Fullerton, Hodgart, and Barclay, of Paisley. As soon after signing the contract as possible, work was commenced at the contractor's shops at Glasgow on the steel columns for the river piers, as well as upon those portions of the opening span that would first be required at the site.

The whole of the work of this contract, both during manufacture and erection, was executed under the personal supervision of Sir William Arrol, who devoted a large amount of his time to the undertaking. Mr. A. S. Biggart, the manager of the contractor's works at Glasgow, was responsible for the construction of the steelwork, and Mr. John Hunter conducted the commercial portion of the contractor's business at the site. Mr. D. Harris and Mr. D. Muirhead were the foremen in charge of the erection of the steelwork on the north and south sides of the river, and they, with Mr. W. Parry, deserve much credit for the way in which the work has been done. As a result of the care bestowed upon that work, no accident of a serious nature has occurred in connection with the building of this portion of the bridge. Many hundreds of men have been employed on the erec-

tion of the steelwork for the last four years, a considerable proportion of whom have steadily laboured throughout the whole time to bring the work to a successful conclusion.

Staging.—The construction of a substantial stage between the shore and the pier on each side of the river was the first portion of the work commenced at the site. This stage, which was 80ft. wide, was made of sufficient strength to carry the whole of the permanent work of the side spans, as well as the plant required for building purposes. No staging which occupied more than 40ft. of the 200ft. waterway was allowed to be placed between the two river piers, as, by Act of Parliament, a clear width of 160ft. had always to be maintained for the river traffic. Two timber dolphins were constructed between each of the abutments and the adjacent pier on each side of the river. These were formed by driving piles well into the ground and securely bracing them together. Upon these, steel lattice girders, generally 5ft. in depth, were placed, and the whole area floored over with 12in. by 6in. timbers and 8in. planking. The formation of this stage occupied some months, as the work was rendered difficult by the large amount of shipping continually passing up and down the river; and although it was necessarily very costly, it was considered indispensable for the successful execution of the contract, not only for the purposes of erection, but also on account of the very limited area of ground available for the storage of material. The temporary girders were so arranged that the three outer ones on each side of this stage would carry the permanent suspension chains when these came to be built, while the four inner girders would be used for supporting the cross girders forming the floor of the side spans. When these stages were completed, rails for travelling cranes were laid along them, extending over the whole length of the approaches to the bridge, so that the material as it arrived at the site could be conveniently placed until the time arrived for it to be erected. A considerable amount of staging, as previously stated, had already been used for building the two piers in the river, and this was taken over by the contractor for the steelwork, but the portion in the waterway between the piers was removed as soon as possible, in order that the river traffic should not be interfered with to a greater extent than was absolutely necessary.

Conveyance of material.—As the steelwork was constructed in Glasgow, it was despatched to London by the steamers of the Clyde Shipping and Carron Companies. The vessels of both these companies discharged their cargoes within half a mile of the bridge into the contractor's barges, and it was then conveyed to either side of the river as required. The quantity sent forward from time to time depended, of course, on the amount finished at the works in Glasgow, but was generally from 50 to 100 tons a week. As much riveting as possible was done before the steelwork was despatched to London, but for the convenience of handling, the weight of any one piece was limited to about five tons. Material urgently required was frequently sent to the site by train.

THE ERECTION OF THE STEELWORK.

Opening span.—After the holding-down bolts on the shore side of the two piers were put into position and

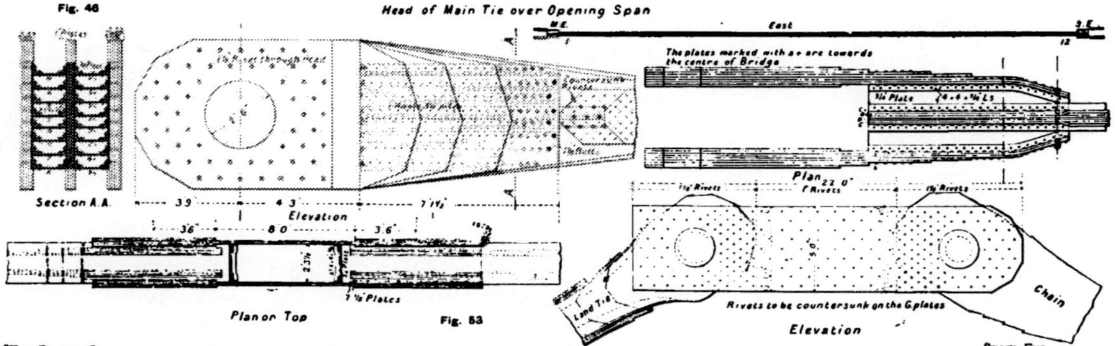
Fig. 46
Head of Main Tie over Opening Span
East
The plates marked with a + are towards the centre of Bridge
Plan
22 0"
Section A.A.
Elevation
Plan or Top
Fig. 53
Rivets to be countersunk on the G plates
Elevation
Chain
Land Tie

"The Engineer" Swain Eng.

Figs. 46 and 53—ENDS OF MAIN HIGH-LEVEL TIE AND LINKS OVER ABUTMENTS

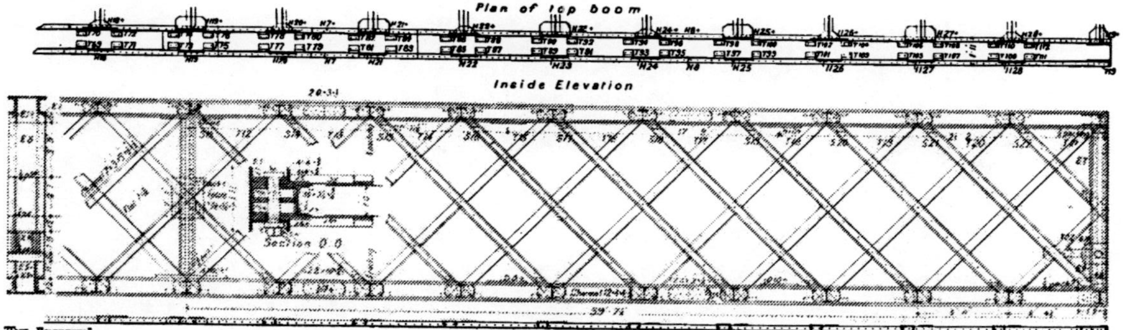
Plan of top boom
Inside Elevation
Section O.O
39' 7¼"

"The Engineer" Swain Eng.

Fig. 48—CENTRAL GIRDERS OF HIGH-LEVEL FOOTWAYS

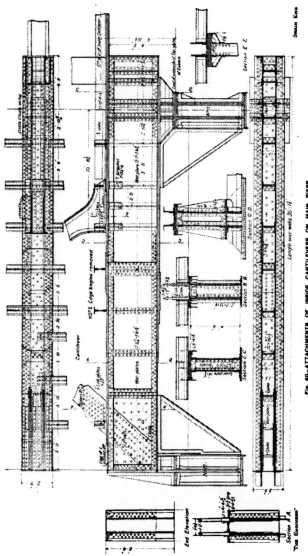

Fig. 40—ATTACHMENTS OF INSIDE CANTILEVERS ON MAIN PIERS

connected to the anchorages that had already been built in the piers, the girders, J and K—Fig. 19, Plate III.— were erected immediately over their ultimate positions, being kept sufficiently high to allow of the lower flanges being riveted. As soon as these girders were built, they were lowered down on to the granite bed-stones, which had been previously covered with three layers of canvas thoroughly coated with red lead, and, to insure them bearing over the whole area of their bottom flanges, red lead was afterwards forced beneath them under considerable pressure. The holding-down bolts were afterwards subjected to a tension of five tons per square inch of sectional area, and while they were thus stressed, the nuts at their upper ends were screwed down until they were bearing hard upon the girders, the bolts still retaining the initial tension. The girders H on the river side of the piers were built above their final positions in the same manner, and afterwards lowered down to within 1in. of the granite bed-stones, this space being then filled with Portland cement grout. The curved cantilevers seen in Fig. 20, Plate III., for supporting the face of the pier against any pressure likely to be caused by passing vessels colliding with it were next erected in place and attached to the girders H. The eight fixed

adopted to insure the bases bearing over their whole area. The second length of the column plates was next put into position by cranes placed upon the piers; but before the third length could be added, the cranes had to be fixed on the top of timber trestles 40ft. in height. In building the columns it was found most convenient to erect all the vertical angle bars first, next to add the horizontal diaphragms which occur about every 8ft., Fig. 22a, and lastly to put the skin plates in position. In cases where the sides consisted of two or more plates these were riveted together in the contractor's yard before being sent to the site. The riveting that had to be done after the columns were erected was all handwork; the men standing upon a small stage surrounding each column, which could easily be raised or lowered by tackle, as required. It rarely happened that more than one squad of men worked upon a stage at one time; but a good squad was able to put in about two hundred $\frac{7}{8}$in. rivets in a day of ten hours. A good deal of care was required to keep the columns plumb while they were being built; and in some cases wire guy ropes were necessary to keep them vertical while they were being riveted.

After the girders forming the first landings were in position, the cranes were placed upon them for continuing

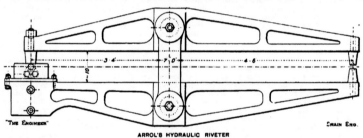

ARROL'S HYDRAULIC RIVETER

girders F—page 85—carrying the main pivot shaft A, which supports the moving leaves, as well as the pinion shafts D for rotating the same, rest upon the top of the girders above referred to. They were built in pairs upon staging resting upon the bottom of the bascule chambers, and, on being completed, were drawn to their places, and secured by turned bolts or rivets, thus leaving the stage clear for the erection of the next pair. The total weight of the steelwork forming the opening span, but not including the moving leaves, is about 850 tons.

Columns on piers.—The bases for each of the columns on the piers—see Fig. 27, pages 58—59—were built about 3ft. above their final places upon timber blocking. The three horizontal sets of plates were first laid down and partly riveted, and the diaphragms were added afterwards. A large amount of the riveting was of a very difficult nature, and special hinged hydraulic riveting machines— see engraving, page 85—having a 4½ft. gap, were made by the contractor to do the work. After most of the diaphragms were in place, the first length of the column plates was put in position and the riveting sufficiently completed to enable the bases to be lowered on to their granite bed-stones, upon which three layers of specially prepared canvas had been placed, and other precautions

the erection of the columns sufficiently to permit of the second landing being built. This landing in its turn served for a support for the cranes, which when placed upon it were able to complete the columns to the top. The girders forming the—see Fig. 22b, page 53—first landings were built upon the piers, under their final positions, and when sufficiently finished, were raised into place by tackle and riveted to the columns. These four main girders being in position, the smaller girders and floor-plates were added, and the whole riveted. The girders of the second landing were erected upon the first landing, and afterwards lifted into their places in the same manner. As the girders which connect the columns together at the top, and form the third landing—see Fig. 22c, page 59—are of considerable weight, timber staging was erected over the main girders of the second landing, so that they could be built and riveted in place. In all these of these floors there are rectangular openings near the east and west columns, through which the cages of the hydraulic lifts will ascend and descend. There are also openings for the stairs through each of the landings —see Figs. 24, 25, and 26, Plates III. and V.

The four columns on each pier are rigidly braced together to resist the wind pressure to which the towers are exposed. The bracing consists of one or more flat steel plates according to the section required, but where such would interfere with the opening for the lower roadway through the columns, curved struts, shown in Fig. 28, Plate III., have been adopted. The bottom portion of these struts was made with the bases of the columns to which they are attached. The upper part is fixed to a horizontal girder, placed at the level of the second landing, and riveted at each end to the columns. These girders were first erected and riveted, the upper portion of the curved struts being then suspended from them, and the remainder gradually built downwards, until they met the portions already constructed at the bases of the columns. Hand riveting was generally used for this work, although where it was possible to get a machine to work, hydraulic riveting was adopted.

It being desirable to have an initial tension of about three and a-half tons per square inch on the flat ties after they were riveted to the columns, the rivet holes in the ties were not drilled exactly opposite those in the gusset plates which attached them to the columns, but in such a position that when the ties were subjected to a tension of the above amount they would coincide. When the holes were thus drilled, everything being ready to rivet the connections, the ties were heated throughout their length, either by Lucigen lamps or ordinary gas, so that the expansion of the metal brought the holes fair. The rivets were then put in and closed by machine, the heat being applied to the ties throughout the whole operation.

The large masonry arch through which the roadway passes from the side spans to the opening portion of the bridge is carried by a series of girders and ties from the columns, as shown in Fig. 46, page 85, and does not rest, as it appears to do, on the fixed girders of the opening span, which are directly beneath it. This arrangement was adopted because fears were entertained lest the vibration attending the opening and shutting of the bridge might be deleterious to the masonry, and it would therefore be better that the arch should be carried by girders not in any way connected with the moving leaves. Stairs made of light steel angles and plates are provided from the level of the lower roadway to the top of the towers. These were constructed at the contractor's works in Glasgow and sent to the site in sections, completely riveted and ready to be put into place. Mason's patent treads have been fixed to these stairs throughout. These treads are made with thin chilled steel plates, in which recesses of dove-tail section are filled with lead. The steel affords great resistance to wear, while the lead gives a good foothold.

The partitions round the lift cases and stairs on the landings are formed by a series of uprights spaced about 5ft. apart, composed of two steel channel bars, riveted together back to back, with occasional horizontal bracing of the same section between them ; the rectangular spaces thus formed are filled in with wooden panels. At a height of some 28ft. above the top of the pier columns, a series of girders are placed to carry the steel principals of the roofs. These girders were all built in place on staging resting on the top landing. They are supported by built-up steel stanchions placed over each of the columns.

High-level footways.—When the columns on the piers were completely built, and the top landing girders all fixed in place, the erection of the high-level footways was commenced. These footways, each of which has a clear width of 12ft., are composed of cantilevers projecting 59ft. beyond the columns—Fig. 47, page 79 and Fig. 40, page 73—between the ends of which central girders 118¾ft. long are suspended—Fig. 48, page 71. The cantilevers bear upon the columns over the opening span, and are securely anchored down to those on the shore side of each pier. The whole of the steel work composing these footways was built across the river on the overhang system, the erection of the cantilevers and girders proceeding from the top of the columns on each pier simultaneously, until the two halves met over the centre of the opening span—Fig. 41-4, pages 45-49. This work was carried out in the following manner :—Cranes were placed upon the top landings for raising the material from the level of the main stage and depositing it within reach of other cranes used for building. The portion of the cantilevers immediately over the top landings was first erected, and when this was riveted the first length projecting over the river was added, each part, as it was put into place, being securely bolted to that which had been already built. The small building cranes were then removed from the landing and placed upon travelling stages resting on the top of this overhanging portion, and in this position they were able to put the various parts composing the next length in position. No difficulty was experienced in carrying out this work, but great care was needed to prevent such articles as rivets, bolts, and light tools from falling upon the vessels continually passing up and down the river. These overhanging portions of the footways being riveted, or thoroughly bolted up, the travelling stages with their cranes were drawn forward about 20ft., so as to be in position for erecting the next length. In this way the cantilevers were gradually built out to the end, and it became necessary to make the junction between them and the central girders. As these girders are only supported from the cantilevers by suspension links, additional attachments were necessary in order that they might be erected in the same manner as the cantilevers. After the suspension links were in place, the end posts of the girders were put into position, and the first length of the bottom booms added. While these were supported by the cranes, iron blocks were inserted in the space between them and the lower booms of the cantilevers.

Some of the diagonal tie bars were next fixed, and these secured the projecting boom of the girders to the upper part of the end post, which was itself temporarily fastened to the cantilevers. The first lengths of the top booms were then put into place, bolted to the end posts, and supported by some of the permanent diagonal struts. A temporary connection was finally made between these booms and the upper booms of the cantilevers by means of steel plates 30in. wide, 12ft. long, and ⅜in. thick. These plates were sufficiently strong to take the stress caused by the weight of the half-length of the central girders, as well as that due to the weight of staging and plant placed upon them, the compressive stress on the lower boom being transferred to the cantilevers through the iron blocks previously referred to.

Having thus constructed the first portion of the central girders, the stage and crane were drawn forward so as to rest upon it, and be in position for building the

Fig. 73—THE MIDDLESEX PIER FROM THE SCUTH—OPENING SPAN

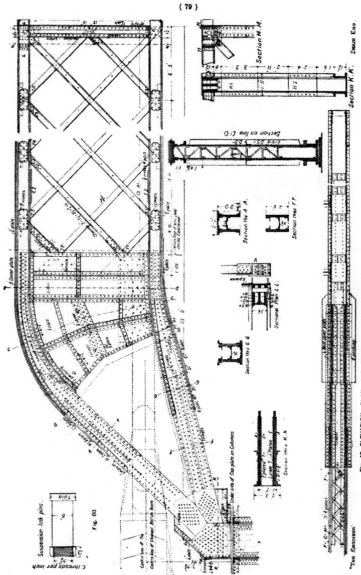

Fig. 47. ELEVATION, PLAN, AND SECTIONS OF OUTSIDE CANTILEVER CARRYING HIGH-LEVEL FOOTWAY

are on the shore side of the pivot shafts, were constructed on the main stage close to the piers. Each of these portions when built weighed from fifty to sixty tons. The lower flanges were first placed on trestles of varying height to suit their curvature, and one of the webs added. The flanges were then riveted by machine, but most of the riveting through the web was hand work. As soon as all the internal diaphragms were in place the second webs were built, and afterwards the top flanges were put into

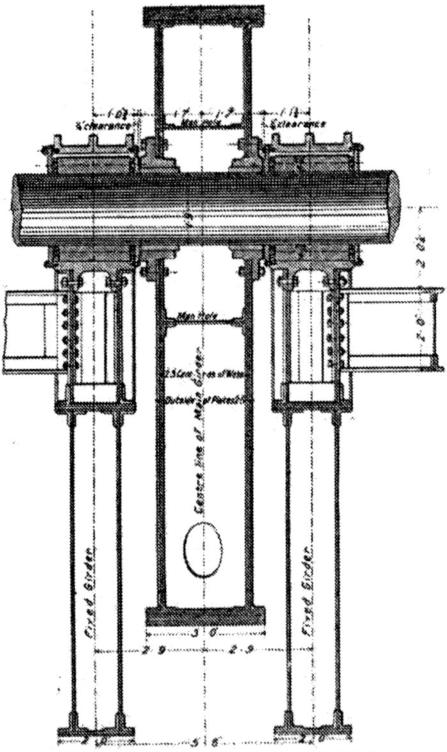

Fig. 50—Cross Section showing Bearings of Main Shaft

position and the riveting completed. The trestles were now removed from beneath, and the girders lowered on to trolleys running on rails laid along the stage. Launching ways had already been fixed in the bascule chambers, and cradles prepared to receive the front part of the girders as they were drawn forward. The large hole in the webs of these girders, which had been bored for the pivot shaft, was then brought opposite the permanent bearings for that shaft, which were already in place on the fixed girders, and a temporary mandril inserted

The launching ways being removed, the shore ends of the girders were gradually lowered to the bottom of the bascule chamber.

The main pivot shafts—Fig. 50 below, and Plates III. and IV.—on which the moving leaves turn, are each 21in. diameter and 48ft. long. These shafts, which weigh about 25 tons, had already been placed on the piers in a line with the bearings, ready to be drawn into position as soon as the four main girders were in place. When the four moving girders—Figs. 49 and 59, Plates III. and IV.—had all been launched forward and turned to an upright position, and securely blocked up underneath, the temporary mandrils were withdrawn and the pivot shafts rolled forward, through the large holes in the webs of the girders, so as to rest upon the permanent supports on the fixed girders —F, Fig. 20, Plate III. The cast steel bearings between the webs of the girders and the shafts were then put into place and secured, and the keys inserted for fixing the shafts to them. Directly the girders had been blocked up at the bottom of the bascule chambers, a length was added to the portion projecting above the pivot. When circumstances arose which rendered it desirable to rotate the leaves for testing purposes during the construction of the bridge, the height that could be built above the pivot was limited to 58ft., as by Act of Parliament no portion of the temporary or permanent work was allowed to project over the central span that would reduce the clear water-way at this level by more than 40ft. All work was consequently suspended upon the upper portion of the girders until the time arrived when it was no longer necessary to experimentally rotate the leaves.

Considerable difficulty was experienced in fixing the quadrants—Fig. 21, Plate III.—to the two outer girders, owing to the confined space in which the work had to be done. As the racks for rotating the leaves are fixed to these quadrants, it was necessary to observe the greatest care in building them in their correct positions, so that the teeth of the racks and those of the pinion shafts should be properly in gear. The quadrants were delivered at the site in large pieces, much of the riveting as possible being done in the contractor's yard. These were lowered into the bascule chamber, and drawn into place by tackle. When they had been temporarily fixed in position, and before any of their joints had been riveted, arrangements were made for turning the leaves, so that by taking careful measurements at various parts of the quadrants as they passed the pinion shafts—D, Fig. 20, Plate III.—it would be possible to see where any alteration was necessary.

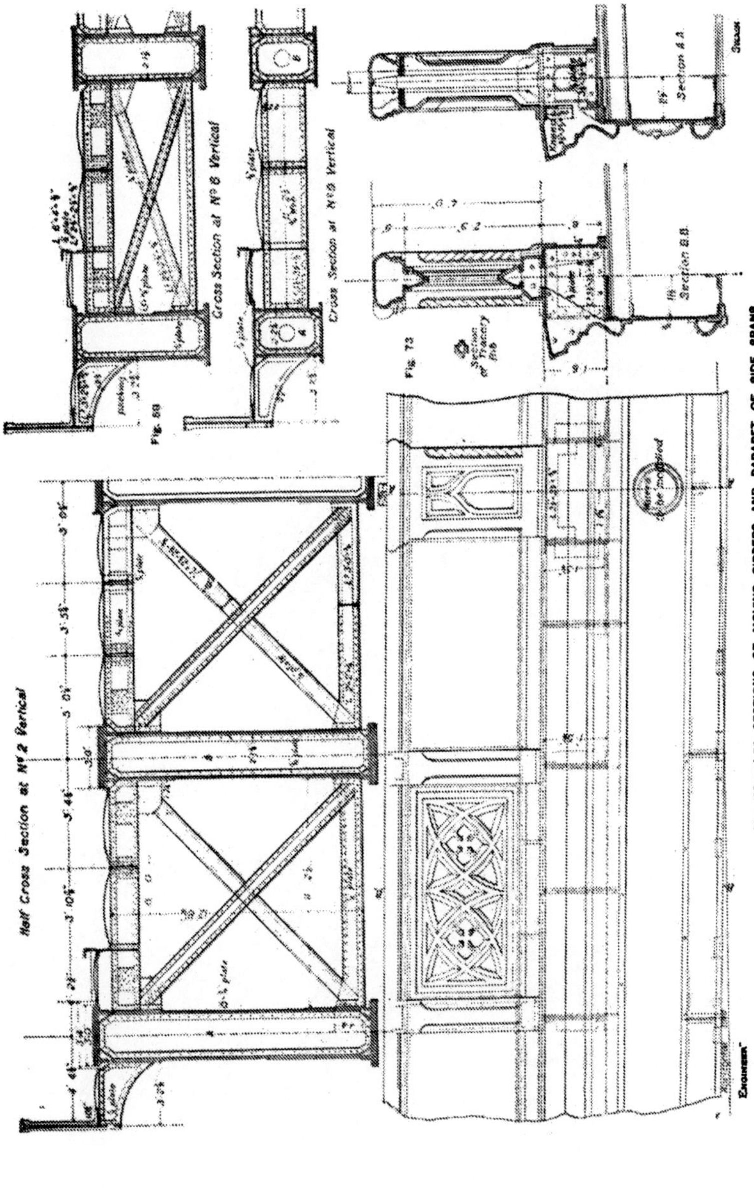

(87)

Figs. 59 and 73 —SECTIONS OF MOVING GIRDERS AND PARAPET OF SIDE SPANS

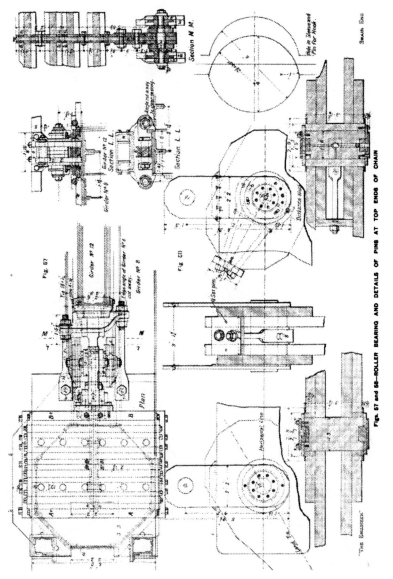

Fig. 57 and 58—ROLLER BEARING AND DETAILS OF PINS AT TOP ENDS OF CHAIN

next length. In this manner the two halves of these girders were built, until they met over the centre of the river, the overhang system of erection being adhered to throughout. As the whole of these footways had been constructed and put together temporarily in the contractor's yard at Glasgow, it was necessary that the first lengths of the central girders should be set in their exact positions so as to insure the two halves just meeting when entirely built. Had the last length of the booms been templated and made to suit the space for which each was intended, no very great care would have been necessary in starting the ends of the girders in their right places, but this final length being already made, the last remaining space between the two halves of the girders had, of course, to be such that the booms just fitted into it. Before fixing the end lengths of the girders, measurements were made across the river, between the extremities of

to the underside of each footway. This stage was necessary for the men engaged upon the riveting of the footways, as well as for those fixing the ornamental castings, but its chief use was to prevent light articles from falling upon the vessels beneath. This last consideration was one of the greatest importance, as the many pleasure steamers, crowded with passengers, continually passing under these footways necessitated the greatest care on the part of the contractors. Fortunately throughout the whole of this portion of the work no accident occurred. When the steelwork was completed, wooden roofs were constructed over each footway, that on the east side of the bridge being so designed that it would contain the cast iron pipes which supply the pressure to the hydraulic engines on the north pier for opening and shutting the bridge.

High-level ties—Figs. 45 and 46.—These ties, pp. 67-71,

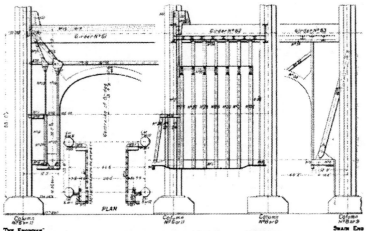

PLAN

THE ENGINEER SWAIN ENG

Fig. 46—STEELWORK SUPPORTING MASONRY ARCH AT PIERS

the cantilever, by means of a steel wire, and the end posts were fixed in such a position that there would be just sufficient space to drop the last booms in their places. When the footways were all constructed with exception of this final length, no difficulty was experienced in inserting the remaining booms, it being only necessary to wait until the temperature was suitable. The operation of joining the two halves together and removing the tie-plates connecting the top booms of the girders and cantilevers together, only occupied about two hours. The iron blocks at the extremities of the lower booms of the cantilevers were afterwards forced out, and the girders were then freely hanging by the permanent suspension rods at their ends. In building the footways out from the piers it was necessary to incline them slightly upward, so that when finished they should have the required camber.

The more important parts of the cantilevers and girders being thus fixed, a light, closely-boarded timber stage, 18ft. wide, extending from pier to pier, was next attached

are 301ft. long and are composed of eight plates, 2ft. wide and 1in. thick. They are suspended about every 15ft. by rods to the upper boom of the outside high level footway girders. Each tie was built upon a stage placed at the top of those columns which are on the shore side of the north pier, and projecting beyond them some 25ft. to 30ft.—Fig. 41. As each length was built and riveted, the ties were drawn by union screws towards the south pier a sufficient distance to allow another length being built on the stage. Owing to the great thickness of the ties it was considered desirable to build and rivet them in two halves, each 4in. thick. When each half was finished they were placed close together, the rivets having been countersunk all along those faces that were to touch, and connected by bolts 1in. diameter spaced about 18in. apart. As the body of each tie was completed the eye-plates were attached to the ends over the north and south piers.

The moving leaves.—The portions of the four main girders of the moving leaves—B, Fig. 20, Plate III.—which

contractor's works at Glasgow, and were afterwards bored out when erected in position, as will be afterwards described. The top eyes being thus secured formed an excellent starting point for the construction of the remainder of these short chains. The upper length of the bottom booms was first put into place and thoroughly bolted up, the lower flange plates being left off until the internal riveting was completed. The second and succeeding lengths were next added, until the whole of these booms were built to the bottom, and connected to the lower eye-plates, which had already been put in position and riveted. This portion of the work being in position,

holes in the eye-plates had been bored to their correct diameters the pins were inserted, but the chains were still supported upon the timber trestles, and by iron packings over the columns on the piers and abutments, and it was not until these packings had been removed, and all the roller bearings put into place over these columns, that the trestles were removed and the chains allowed to hang freely.

Boring pin holes.—As previously mentioned, the holes for the large pins at each end of the chains, as well as those in the horizontal links over the abutment columns, and at the ends of the high-level ties over the pier

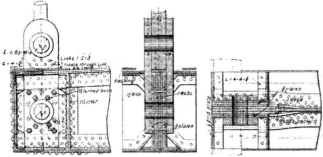

Fig. 60—SUSPENSION OF THE CROSS GIRDERS

the vertical and diagonal web bracing was erected, and finally the top boom was added in lengths, being built downwards from the eye-plates, only the upper flange plates being left off to allow the work to be riveted.

When the erection of the short chains was completed, and the machine riveting finished, the gantry, carrying the steam crane, was drawn towards the pier, so as to be in position for building the middle and lower portions of the long chains. The higher trestles for supporting the chains were then securely braced to the gantry, which greatly increased the lateral stiffness of the stages. The method of building the long chains was similar in all respects to that adopted in the case of the shorter ones. The top eye-plates were first erected near their final positions by the cranes on the top of the pier columns, and when the riveting had been done, they were drawn into position between the jaws of the high-level ties, temporary mandrils placed in the large pin holes, and the projecting ends of the eye-plates lowered to their proper inclination. The first two lengths of the lower boom were then raised by the same cranes, swung into position, and securely bolted to these eye-plates. The third and remaining portions of this boom were put into place by the crane on the gantry. When some riveting, which could not have been done afterwards was finished, the vertical and diagonal web bracing was erected, and finally the top boom was added, being built downwards from the top eye-plates. All parts of the steel work which could not be painted after the work was riveted were coated with Portland cement, and the upper booms of all the chains were entirely filled with coke breeze concrete before the top flange plates were put in place. When the large pin

columns, were bored before leaving the contractor's works to within ¼in. of their final diameters. When these various members of the bridge were erected at the site, and all the portions forming a joint were together, the holes were in all cases bored to their correct sizes. The labour thus entailed was equivalent to boring a hole 2ft. 6in. in diameter through 65ft. of solid steel. As this

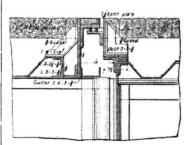

Fig. 63—EXPANSION JOINT SIDE SPAN FLOORS

boring had to be done over the tops of the columns on the piers and abutments, besides at various other places, it was necessary to provide boring bars, engines, and boilers, that could be transferred from one position to another and easily fixed where required.

A great deal of time was occupied in fixing the boring

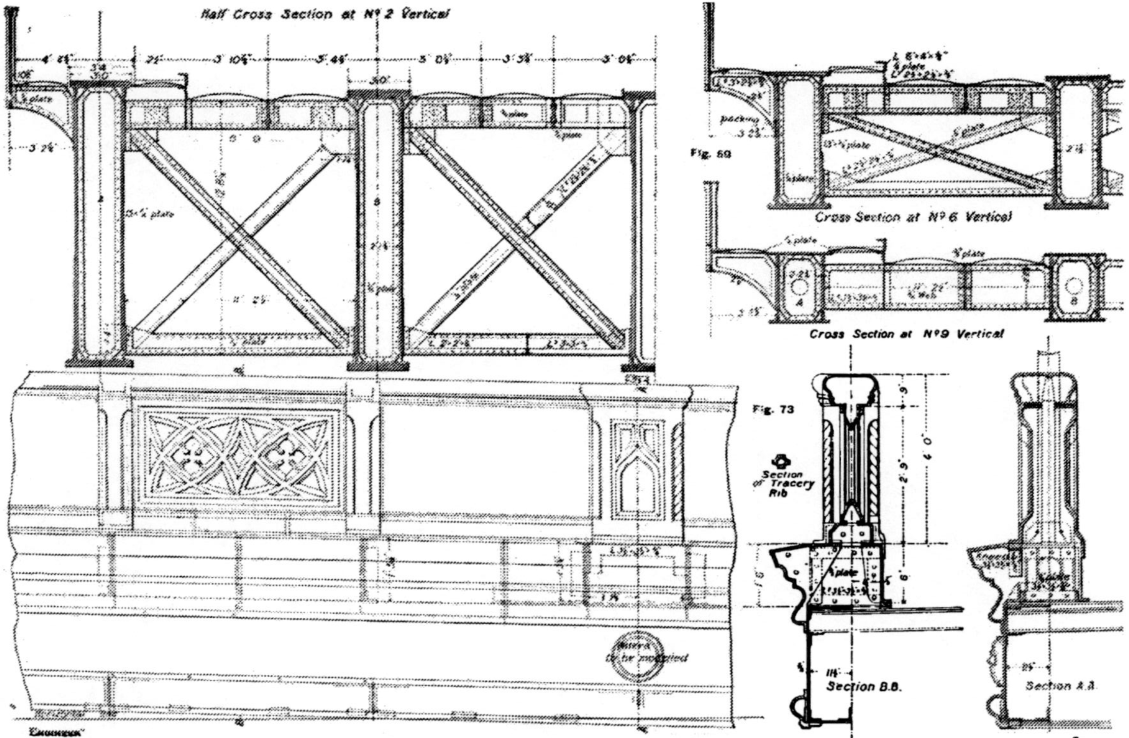

Fig. 69 and 73—SECTIONS OF MOVING GIRDERS AND PARAPET OF SIDE SPANS

Fig. 63—ACCUMULATOR HOUSE—VIEW FROM SOUTH-WEST

The leaf as now built, with the two quadrants attached, weighed some 400 tons, and in order to reduce the power that would be required to lift the lower end of the girders, it was just balanced about the main pivot shafts by attaching thirty-seven tons of lead near the end of the upper portion of the leaf. The rotation of the leaf, which was easily effected by means of a small steam winch fixed upon the main stage, was repeatedly stopped to allow the measurements being made between the quadrants and the pinion shafts. From these observations it was apparent that the radius of the quadrants would require slight adjustment before the racks could be fixed to them. This work was commenced at once, and when the necessary corrections had been made, the leaf was again rotated to ascertain if sufficient accuracy had been obtained. This examination proving satisfactory, the quadrants were riveted to the girders and entirely finished. Arrangements were now made for scribing lines along the centre and edges of the flange plate of the quadrants, and for this purpose steel scribers were fixed at a known distance from the pinions, the leaves were again lowered, and the lines carefully marked. The racks were now fixed in their correct positions, as indicated by these lines, and it was only necessary to slightly pack or chip them to neutralise any little inequalities occurring in the work.

Columns on abutments. — The erection of the steel columns on the north and south abutments—see Figs. 51 and 52, pages 61 and 37—was commenced when those over the piers were little more than half built. The girders forming the bases of these columns were first constructed and riveted over their ultimate places, and afterwards lowered to within 1in. of the granite bed stones, this space being subsequently filled with Portland cement grout. The columns, which are similar to, but of smaller diameter than, those over the piers were next built, and the lattice bracing connecting those on the east and west sides of the bridge fixed in position. The bracing on the north and south sides of each set of abutment columns is composed of plate box girders, the underside of which is curved. The portions of this bracing attached to the columns were first built, so as to project such a distance that the central part could be put into place between them. Owing to the connection required for the stiffening girders, the bases of the Surrey abutment are somewhat different in construction from those on the north side of the river. The columns were chiefly riveted by hand, but hydraulic riveting was almost entirely adopted for the bases.

Horizontal links.—The links which connect the land ties and the short chains over the abutment columns—Fig. 58, page 71 and Plate III.—are similar on both sides of the river. These links are supported by roller bearings over each column, but they were temporarily carried during erection upon iron packings, sufficient space being left to place the permanent bearings in position at a later date. They are composed of steel plates, 22ft. to 28ft. long, 5ft. to 5½ft. wide, and ⅞in. thick, placed side by side and riveted together, the connection between these links and the land ties and chains being made by pins, varying in diameter between 21in. and 30in.

Land ties.—On the north side of the river the land ties—Fig. 54, page 67—are connected to the anchorage girder by pins 2ft. in diameter. Below the road level each tie is composed of twelve plates, 21in. wide and

½in. thick, and was built and riveted in two halves in order to avoid the use of very long rivets. The two halves being completed, they were brought close together, the rivets having been countersunk along those faces which were to touch each other, and connected by bolts 1in. diameter, spaced about 18in. apart. The portion of the ties above the road, being unsupported between the level of the ground and the top of the abutment columns, is altered in form so as to be better able to resist the bending stress caused by its own weight. This part of each tie was built in place, upon staging, and before the top boom was put into position the space between the two webs was entirely filled with coke-breeze concrete, it being impossible to keep this internal portion of the steelwork painted after completion. On the south side of the river, the upper portion of these ties is similar to that above described, but the part below the road level is composed of twelve flat plates, 33in. wide, by ⅝in. thick, secured to the anchorage girder by rivets. Special bearings are provided for all ties at the roadway, and the portions below this level are also supported at frequent intervals.

The chains.—It was always considered that building the chains—see Plates III., IV., and V.—which support the floor of the side spans, would be an operation of considerable difficulty, and one requiring great care and attention. The staging, for supporting them during erection, owing to its height and exposed position, had to be carefully designed, and special arrangements had also to be devised for raising and putting into place the many parts of which these chains are composed. As already mentioned, the girders under the main stage, between the abutments and piers, were so arranged that the three outer ones on each side would support the weight of the chains during erection, the four remaining girders being intended to carry the permanent cross girders and floor of these side spans. Over these three outside girders, therefore, timber trestles were placed about 18ft. apart. The tops of these trestles were connected together by 12in. by 6in. longitudinal timbers, closely covered with 3in. planking, forming a platform about 10ft. wide, sufficient space for working being allowed between it and the lower boom of the chains. The weight of the chains being about one ton per foot run, the whole of this staging had to be constructed in a very substantial manner, and thoroughly braced together in all directions.

On referring to Fig. 19, Plate III., it will at once be seen that only a small portion of the chains could be built by cranes, placed on the columns over the piers and abutments. It was therefore considered desirable to construct a travelling gantry—shown on Plate V.—about 84ft. high, capable of carrying a steam crane, which, with a jib between 60ft. and 70ft. in length, would command all parts of the work beyond the reach of those cranes on the columns. The shorter chains on both sides of the river were the first to be commenced. The upper eye-plates were built as near to their ultimate positions as possible; and when the necessary riveting had been done, they were drawn into place between the horizontal links over the abutment columns. A temporary mandril was then put through the large pin holes, and the projecting ends of the eye-plates were gradually lowered to their correct inclination. The whole of the large pin holes were bored to within ⅛in. of their final diameters before leaving the

Fig. 83 – THE NORTHERN MAIN PIER – MASONRY SUPERSTRUCTURE, NOVEMBER, 1893

Fig. 78 – THE SOUTHERN MAIN PIER MASONRY SUPERSTRUCTURE, OCTOBER, 1893

Select Committee which passed the Bill for this bridge, that the average number of vessels which would require the bridge to be opened was about twenty-two in twenty-four hours. Allowing five minutes for each, this would cause the bridge only to be open for the river traffic for about two hours each day. This interruption to the road traffic will chiefly occur at intervals during the two hours before and the two hours after high water. In the event of several vessels passing through the bridge one close behind the other, the leaves would have to be open for more than the five minutes, but it is not expected that vessels would be so numerous as to cause the bridge to remain open longer than fifteen to twenty minutes at any one time. Special lamps have been fixed at each end of each pier to indicate at night whether the bridge is open or shut.

The estimated annual cost of working the bridge has been calculated on the following basis:—The expense of working the machinery would amount to £1600. This item would include the wages of two bridge-masters, one by day and one by night, two engine-drivers, two firemen, four men on the bridge, and the men for working the hoists; it also includes coal and stores. The police would cost, assuming eight men were sufficient for regulating the traffic, £540; and cleansing, watering, and lighting, £624. Allowing £700 for repairs and painting the bridge, the cost thus amounts to £3464 a year. This does not allow anything for the depreciation of the machinery, which, if taken at 2 per cent., would bring the total annual cost of working the bridge up to £5168.

The general arrangement of the machinery is shown on Plate V. Four boilers, each 30ft. long and 7½ft. in diameter, are placed in two of the arches forming the southern approach to the bridge. The adjacent arch is utilised as a coal store, the coal being delivered by barges brought alongside the south abutment, and afterwards conveyed to the store by small trucks, running on a narrow-gauge line of rails especially laid for this purpose. In the two following arches of the approach, to the south of that used for the coal store, are placed the pumping engines for supplying the hydraulic pressure. It was originally intended that the water which is forced by these engines into the accumulators should be drawn from the Thames, as is done at the various stations of the Hydraulic Supply Company, as well as at the docks along the river; but as the water is also used over and over again, there being a return pipe from the engines and lifts on the piers, this idea was abandoned, and water from the ordinary supply is used. Each of the pumping engines has four steam cylinders of 38in. stroke, two of which are 19in. diameter for high-pressure, and two 37in. diameter for low pressure. Each of the two hydraulic pumps attached to either engine has a plunger 7½in. diameter, the stroke being also 38in. These engines make forty-five revolutions per minute.

The accumulator house—page 89 and Plate V.—has been built on the east side of the southern approach near the pumping engines. It contains two 20in. accumulators, each loaded to give a pressure from 700 to 800 lb. per sq. in. The water is conveyed from these to the machinery for opening the leaves on the piers through two 6in. pipes. These are laid under the footpath on the east side of the side span, special flexible joints being made both at the pier and abutment, and also at the junction of the two chains, so that they may conform to any movements occasioned by

alteration of temperature and unequal loading to which the bridge may be subjected. From the south pier the water is conveyed by pipes placed inside one of the steel columns, up to the east high-level footway, and continued along the top of the cantilevers and girders, over the central span, to one of the columns on the north pier, inside which similar pipes are placed for conveying it to the engines for opening the leaf on this side of the river. After the water has been used, it is returned to the pumping engines by a 7in. pipe. There are two distinct hydraulic engines at each end of each pier for opening and shutting the bridge. It will be noticed on referring to Fig. 86, that at each pier there are two separate pinion shafts geared into the racks that are attached to the quadrants, the engines at one end of a pier working the upper and those at the other end the lower of these shafts.

Each of the two hydraulic engines at either end of a pier has three cylinders, the diameter of their pistons being in one case 7½in., and in the other 8½in. The stroke is the same in all cases, and is 12in. These engines can be used separately or together as occasion may require; thus, on a calm day, one would be sufficient to open the bridge, but when the leaves have to be rotated against a considerable wind pressure, it will be necessary to use the two together. The pressure exerted by the pistons of these engines is increased by gearing before it is transmitted to the racks fixed to the quadrants. The number of teeth of the pinions and wheels between the hydraulic engines and the quadrants, commencing at the engines, being as follows : 15, 41, 13, 29, and 13, this last being the pinion which is geared into the racks attached to the quadrants. We have already seen that a wind pressure of 56 lb. per square foot is equivalent to a force of 140 tons acting on a leaf with a leverage of about 56ft. To overcome this resistance, the total force that must be applied to the racks of the quadrants is about 190 tons, to which must be added that force which is necessary to overcome inertia and the friction of the main pivot shaft.

An accumulator with a ram 22in. diameter is placed at each end of each pier, beneath the engines, the two on each pier being connected together by pipes laid along the bottom of the bascule chamber.

The pinions on the shafts that are caused to rotate by the engines at each end of the piers are geared into racks that have been attached along the arc of each quadrant Fig. 74, Plate V. These racks are of cast steel, each being a segment of a circle having a radius at the pitch line of 42ft. They are about 6ft. long and 17in. wide. Two rows of these racks are fixed side by side to each quadrant, the attachment being made by eleven 1½in. turned steel bolts, spaced about 12in. apart. The holes for these bolts were all very carefully drilled after the racks had been accurately set. Much difficulty was experienced in fixing these segments owing to the confined space that was afforded for the men to work in. The two lower pairs—those next to the ballast-box—were first put into their approximate position on each quadrant, and the moving leaf was then lowered until these came into gear with the pinions which were already in position. The lowering of the leaf was then continued, and the pinion shaft rotated, so as to run through the whole of the teeth of these racks. It could thus be seen if the segments were in their true positions, and any necessary corrections could then be made if such

bar and engine in each case, the amount of time expended on this being generally as great as that required to bore the hole. Great accuracy was also required to be observed in boring the holes truly parallel, the actual diameter, however, was not a matter of such great importance, as steel gauges were always made, showing the diameter of the holes, and the pins were turned to suit in all cases, about $\frac{1}{16}$th of an inch play generally being allowed. In addition to boring the holes for the pins, holes had also to be bored through the webs of the eight fixed girders on each pier, to form bearings for the pinion shafts D—Fig. 20, Plate III., and Fig. 65, p. 99—for opening the moving leaves of the centre span. As each of the girders has two webs there were sixty-four holes to bore, varying in diameter from 17in. to 32in., the total thickness of metal to be bored through being 10ft. As a general rule after the boring bar and engine had been fixed in place, the boring of a hole was continued night and day until the work was completed. The different members to be bored at one time had always to be rigidly fixed together, so that the expansion and contraction of the steelwork, due to any alteration of temperature during the operation of boring, should not prevent the hole being truly circular.

Suspension rods.—The diameter of the suspension rods for hanging the floor of the side spans to the chains is either 5½in. or 6in., according to their length. These rods were all forged, their ends being afterwards machined. Each rod is jointed near its centre by means of a screw coupling—Fig. 67, page 43. Consequently, the levels of the cross girders could be adjusted with the greatest accuracy in every case. As each rod was entirely finished it was tested by being subjected to a tension of two hundred tons before it left the contractor's yard.

Floor of side spans.—The cross girders—Fig. 70, page 43—attached to the bottom of the suspension rods were built and riveted on the approaches to the bridge, and afterwards placed on trolleys and run into their positions as required. Each girder is about 61ft. long, 2ft. 3½in. deep at the centre, and weighs about 22 tons. They are connected to the suspension rods at each end by pins 6in. in diameter—see Fig. 68, page 79, and Fig. 69, page 92—passing through a pair of links attached to the cross girders. As these girders were brought into place one by one, the longitudinal girders were riveted to them, and the corrugated floor-plates afterwards put into position. These floor-plates, which are ⅜in. thick, vary in length between 15ft. and 23ft., and were stamped by the contractor to the required form. Owing to the movements caused by alterations of temperature, special joints are made in the flooring of these side spans at the abutments and piers, as well as at the cross girder, which is suspended immediately under the junction of the chains. These joints are shown in Figs. 68, page 92.

Roller bearings on columns.—Roller bearings for supporting the chains are placed on each of the columns on the shore side of the river piers, as well as on those columns on the river side of each of the abutments; and similar bearings are also placed on the other columns on each abutment, for supporting the upper ends of the land ties. The rollers in each case rest upon steel plates 3in. thick, riveted to the top of the columns. The upper surface of these plates was prepared with the greatest care, so that it might be as nearly flat as possible, in order that the rollers should bear evenly throughout

their entire length. A general idea of these bearings can be formed by referring to Figs. 57, page 105, from which it will be seen that the class of work was of a very complex character, requiring great care and considerable time to accomplish.

Pins.—The pins at the ends of the chains and land ties are shown in Fig. 58, page 88. These pins were all forged approximately to shape, and afterwards turned to their correct diameters as given by the gauges made from the finished holes. About $\frac{1}{16}$in. play was allowed between the pin and the hole. The sleeves which surround the pins were made either by forging hollow steel ingots upon a mandril, or boring a hole through a solid ingot nearly equal in diameter to the pins for which the sleeves were being made. The ring thus formed was then parted longitudinally, afterwards turned and bored to the exact size required, and finally again parted to form the two half sleeves. Grooves are cut along the pins so that they can be lubricated at any time, special pumps being used for forcing in the lubricant under great pressure.

Roadway over the bridge.—The roadway of the side spans was formed by filling up the corrugated floor plates with concrete, the upper surface of which was made slightly convex, and prepared for the ordinary wood paving blocks. The side-walks are paved with patent Victoria stone throughout. A cross section of the roadway of these spans is given in Fig. 71, Plate III. The flooring over the moving portion of the bridge is formed by entirely covering the leaf with creosoted Memel timber the underside of which was shaped to fit the curvature of the buckled plates. On this timber packing, greenheart planks, 15in. to 18in. wide by 9in. thick, were laid close together, and over these the patent wood paving blocks of the Acmé Flooring Company were laid, the whole of the woodwork being securely fixed to the buckled plates by bolts. The general arrangement of this flooring is shown with the engravings relating to hydraulic arrangements, Fig. 72, Plate V. The footpath along the high-level footways has been made by covering the steel floor plates with a few inches of metallic concrete.

The stiffening girders.—These girders are placed under the short chains on the southern side span, and connect the large pins, at the junction of the two chains, to the bases of the abutment columns, which are securely fixed by the masonry which surrounds them. The general arrangement of these girders is shown in Fig. 60, page 81. The large hole for the pin at each end of these girders was bored to its true size after all the work was erected, and before the staging which supported the junction of the chains was removed.

Anchor girders.—Each of the land ties on the north side of the river is connected by a pin 2ft. in diameter to an anchorage girder 40ft. long, 4ft. wide and 4ft. deep. The similar girders on the south side are 50ft. long, 4½ft. wide and 4ft. deep, the land ties are, however, riveted to the girders on this side of the river instead of having a pin connection. The tension exerted by the ties is resisted by the weight of the large mass of concrete that surrounds the girders. A means of access to the anchorages has been provided.

Ornamental castings.—Cast iron parapets have been attached along each side of the bridge throughout its entire length. Those fixed along the side spans are shown in Fig. 73, page 85. Similar cast iron parapets are also placed along both sides of the northern approach

Fig. 81—MIDDLESEX ABUTMENT, WEST SIDE

Fig. 82—FRONT ELEVATION OF MIDDLESEX ABUTMENT

work of these two contracts. The stone, as it arrived in vessels at the site, was unloaded at the staging near the north and south piers, and afterwards deposited along the approaches to the bridge, but the limited amount of storage room available was the cause of considerable difficulty in this, as well as in other contracts.

The granite for the superstructure was obtained from the Eddystone Granite Quarries, where it was prepared before being shipped, each stone being cut and dressed to suit the position it was to occupy in the structure; Messrs. Brunton and Trier's patent surfacing machines for the plain work, and their turning machines for the circular and moulded work, being extensively used for dressing the surfaces of the stones, thus saving a large amount of hand work.

The masonry which surrounds the two abutments was not commenced until the steelwork which it envelopes was completed. For the purpose of raising and setting the stones, two travelling steam cranes were erected on rails laid along the top of the steelwork in each case; scaffolding was placed round the towers for the men employed upon their construction.

The masonry of the towers over the piers was built in a somewhat similar manner, although very little scaffolding was used until the work was brought up to the level of the top of the steel columns, the men working upon stages that were supported by wire ropes, and which could be raised or lowered as the work required. The lower portion of the masonry was built by means of two travelling steam cranes, placed on rails laid along the steelwork of the first landing, in which position they were able to command all the work below them. As the building proceeded, these cranes were taken down and re-erected on rails laid along the second landing, and were then able to complete the work up to this level. A timber gantry, resting on the top of the footway girders, was next constructed near each pier. This gantry was about 70ft. long, and rails were laid along it for a travelling crane, similar to those already used. This crane was able to raise all the materials required, from one side of each of the piers, and deposit the stones either in or near their final positions.

The east and west sides of each of the two river piers is devoted to the machinery chambers, where the hydraulic machinery for opening and shutting the bridge is placed —see Plate V. These chambers are roofed over with steel joists and plates, on the top of which the footways along the side spans are carried round the towers to the hydraulic lifts and the footpaths over the moving leaves of the bridge. By this arrangement the whole of the space afforded by the main archway over the piers is available for vehicular traffic. These side portions of the piers will, no doubt, form a favourite resort for many people, as from them one of the best views of this part of the Thames can be obtained.

The towers over the two piers are precisely alike, and form the chief feature of the superstructure. At each of the four angles there is a circular turret, about 9ft. in diameter, and rather over a quarter engaged, inside which is an octagonal space occupied by one of the steel columns—Fig. 79 and 80, page 93.

Each tower is divided into four stages, divided from each other by broad bands of plain masonry, further accentuated by string courses above and below. The ground storey is principally occupied by the large arch spanning the roadway—see Fig. 84, page 101—85ft. span, 16ft. in height at the springing, and 31ft. to the apex. It is ornamented on each face with bold mouldings, the side facing the land span of the bridge having buttresses of two stages, gabled, and ornamented on the face with a shield, charged with the City arms. Between these buttresses and the circular turrets are the entrances to the stairs which lead to the high-level footways. The first dozen steps are of granite, but the remainder of these stairs are constructed of steel, as already described. Above the top of the steel columns a circular cast iron stairway is placed, so that access may be had to the roof over each tower, and to the hydraulic pipes which are situated at this level. On the east and west faces of the towers, at the level of the lower roadway, there are double doorways communicating with the lifts.

The broad band dividing the stages is ornamented over the arch with the arms of the City, and traceried panels. Immediately above this are three windows, the centre of five lights, subdivided horizontally by two transoms, and a window slightly lower than the centre one of three lights, with one transom only on either side—Fig. 79. Flanking the whole, on the front facing the land span are two canopied niches, with elaborate vaulting in the canopies. This feature is omitted on the opposite side of the tower facing the central span.

The third stage has one five-light four-centred window in the middle, doubly transomed, and with a balcony corbelled out about 4ft. from the wall face. The window is flanked by pinnacles, and on either side by two smaller windows of two lights, square - headed, and having single transoms. The fourth stage has four two-light windows, square-headed, with balcony on the side facing the land span, but only two windows of similar character, without balconies, facing the river span. At this stage the angle turrets are corbelled out and become octagonal in form, finishing above in four large pinnacles, with angle rolls and finials. This fourth stage is finished with an embattled parapet, with a central feature on each face, two two-light windows under a gable, with finials and crockets on the north and south sides, and single three-light windows with the same features on the east and west sides. The whole is surmounted by a high pitched roof, the framing being wholly of steel, hipped from each angle, ornamented with louvres midway, and finished with an elaborate cast ridge about 19ft. high of open tracery work. The roof itself is covered with slates from Welsh quarries.

The first, second, and third stages on the east and west sides of the towers are also pierced with windows, the first stage having large two-light windows of two stages in the centre, with smaller ones at the sides, and the second and third three windows in each stage—Fig. 80, page 93.

The materials used in the construction of these towers are grey Cornish granite, Portland stone, and brickwork. The walls are of rock-faced granite on the outside, the inside portion being brickwork. The turrets at the angles and the bands of masonry dividing the stages are of ashlar-faced granite, as well as the large arch spanning the roadway, with its buttresses on the land span side of the towers. Portland stone has been used throughout for the windows, the embattled parapet with its central features, and the angle pinnacles above the underside of the parapet.

time the apparatus above alluded to for bringing up the motion of the leaves were to fall, their impact would be taken by these buffers, which would bring them to rest in the same manner as that in which the hydraulic cylinders that are attached to heavy guns take up the recoil. It has been calculated that the energy of recoil of one of the leaves, travelling at a velocity of, say, 5ft. per second at the periphery, would amount to about one-fifth of the energy of recoil exerted by a 100-ton gun fired with its full

speed. There will also be recorded the exact position in which all the accumulators are, so that before the bridge is started the men can tell whether they are charged or not. Indication will also be given whether the bolts which are shot out at the end of one of the leaves to look it is to the other leaf are in their position for locking the bridge, or out of that position. All the levers which actuate the machinery are placed in these cabins.

position in cylinder, which will then cause the chain to be tightened. This little hydraulic cylinder will be in connection with the locking arrangement of the levers in the cabin, so that until the chain is in position across the archway, the men in charge of the machinery will not be able to pull back the bolts at the ends of the moving leaves, and open the bridge.

When vessels requiring to pass through the bridge have given the necessary signal, the moving leaves will

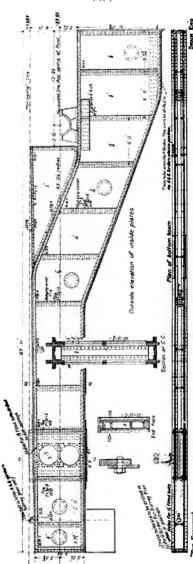

Fig. 65.—FIXED GIRDERS CARRYING MAIN PIVOT SHAFT ON PIERS

charge, and in the case of the gun there is no difficulty in bringing up the recoil within a distance of 4ft.

Cabins have been constructed at the east and west ends of each of the piers for the men who have the control of the machinery for opening and shutting the bridge. In these cabins recording machines will be placed which will indicate exactly the position in which each leaf happens to be at that moment of time, and whether the engines are working, and if so, at what

Before opening the bridge it has been proposed to place a chain across the entrance to each pier for the purpose of stopping the road traffic. These chains will be fixed in place by the policemen stationed at or near them; they will be connected to one side of the archway, and at the other side there will be a small cock, the handle of which will be carried by the man fixing the chain, who will, as soon as he has hooked the chain on, be able to turn the cock, thus allowing the water to enter a small

at once be cleared of all traffic, an operation which it is considered can be performed in one minute. When this is accomplished the leaves will be opened, and it is computed that this will take another minute. Allowing one minute for a vessel to pass through and one minute for closing the bridge, the total time required to open and shut the leaves for letting a vessel through is four minutes, or, say, five minutes, allowing for unavoidable delays. It was stated in the evidence given before the

ment of the staircase, but in all other respects it is similar in character to the one already described. The materials used are the same as in the towers over the piers, and consist of brickwork faced with grey Cornish granite and Portland stone. The latter has been used for the ribs of the arch soffit, and the dressed work of the parapet, including the corbelling, the string course, and the embattled parapet above, the dressings generally of the small windows over the arch, and the large central panels with their carvings and pinnacles. The grey Cornish granite is either rock-faced or ashlar; the former being used in the walls generally, and the latter for all quoins and dressed work other than that already described a Portland stone, and including the mouldings of the large arch and its label terminations, which are carved with the arms of the City on a plain shield with supporters.

The general effect of the masonry superstructure of the bridge is shown in the photographs, pages 93 and 97 which show a front elevation of the Middlesex abutment, looking north, and a side elevation of its west face. The photographs— pages 57 and 65—show a front elevation of the tower over the north pier looking south, and a side elevation of its west face. The general character of the large archways through the Middlesex abutment and through the tower over the northern pier is shown by the sketches, page 101. Stairways leading from the road in front of the Tower of London to the approach to the bridge at the east side of the northern abutment are provided, and a somewhat similar stairway also occurs on the east side of the Surrey abutment.

It will be seen from the photographs—pages 93 and 97 —and description, that a large amount of modelling and carving has been employed throughout the bridge. The whole of this work has been executed by Messrs. Mabey and Son, of Westminster, the work being executed on the ground at the site, or after the masonry was erected in the towers.

It may now be said that the bridge is practically finished. The moving leaves are entirely built, and have been lowered and raised several times by the hydraulic machinery provided for that purpose. The result of

Fig. 62—CITY ARMS, HIGH-LEVEL FOOTWAY

these trials has been in every case most satisfactory. The work that still remains to be done consists chiefly in painting the steelwork of the bridge, and removing the temporary staging that has been used for the erection of the superstructure. This will be completed in June, in which month the bridge will be opened to the public by the Prince and Princess of Wales on behalf of Her Majesty the Queen.

As we have already said, the work was commenced in June, 1886, consequently it has taken eight years to complete the structure.

At first sight one might fancy that this is a long time for the construction of a bridge, but we must remember that the position of the Tower Bridge, situated as it is in the busiest part of the river, made it impossible to build the two piers simultaneously. Frequent delays were also occasioned by the limited amount of staging that could be placed in the river, that the shipping interests might not be interfered with more than was absolutely necessary. The small area of ground available for the storage of materials and plant, and various strikes that occurred during the construction of the bridge also prevented rapid progress.

Besides this bridge, Mr. Barry has carried out many other important works, among which may be mentioned the Barry Dock, near Cardiff—the largest single dock in the United Kingdom — the railways connecting it with the South Wales coalfields, the completion of the Inner Circle Railway joining the Mansion House and Aldgate stations in London, and the widening of the Blackfriars Railway Bridge over the Thames. In 1886 the Government appointed Mr. Barry as a member of the Royal Commission on Irish Public Works, and in 1889 he was nominated by the Board of Trade on a commission ordered by Parliament to settle certain important matters connected with the river Ribble. In the same year he was appointed by the Government on the Western—Scottish—Highlands and Islands Commission, a commission having objects similar to those of the Royal Commission on Irish Public Works. Mr. Barry is a member of the Council of the Institute of Civil Engineers, and consulting engineer for the North-Eastern and Caledonian Railway Companies.

PRINTED BY GEORGE REVEIRS, 4 AND 5, GRAYSTOKE-PLACE, FETTER-LANE, LONDON, E.C.

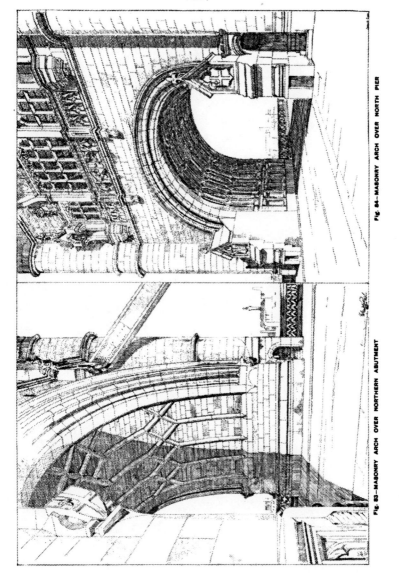

Fig. 84—MASONRY ARCH OVER NORTH PIER

Fig. 83—MASONRY ARCH OVER NORTHERN ABUTMENT

(103)

were not the case, by either inserting thin steel packing pieces between them and the quadrants, or reducing the chipping strips that had been provided at the back of these castings for the purpose of such adjustments.

When all these racks were thus fixed with sufficient accuracy the holes for the turned bolts were bored, and the bolts finally inserted. The next four segments were then attached to each quadrant, the moving leaves were again lowered, until these came into gear with the pinions, which were revolved so as to run through them. The necessary adjustments were then made in the same manner as previously adopted. In this way the whole of the racks were fixed along the arcs of the quadrants. This method of doing the work insured great accuracy, but it occupied considerable time and labour, each of the leaves having to be lowered and raised about six times. The partial rotation of the leaves was not itself a difficult matter, as they had been previously balanced about the main pivot shafts, so that a small steam winch was found to be quite sufficient to do all that was required. When they were in their horizontal position the leaves projected some 20ft. beyond the piers, and the permission of the Conservators had always to be first obtained before the operation of lowering could be commenced, and barges moored in front of each pier to protect the overhanging portion from damage that might have been caused by vessels passing up and down the river.

The main pivot shafts which carry the moving leaves are made of steel. They are each in one piece 48ft. long, 21in. dia., and weigh about twenty-five tons. When the bridge is opened for the river traffic, each of the leaves, weighing nearly

Fig. 61—CENTRAL PANEL, SIDE SPAN PARAPETS

1200 tons, is entirely carried by one of the shafts, which is supported on the fixed girders, at each side of the four main girders forming a leaf. These bearings are shown in Fig. 50. Circular steel castings are attached to each of the two webs of the main girders, through which the shaft passes, and to which it is keyed. Live rollers are placed round the shaft at each of these bearings to reduce the friction as much as possible. When the shafts were delivered at the site they were taken forward to the piers and placed in a line with the bearings, so that when the main girders were in place they could be rolled forward into their final positions.

Each of the pinion shafts is in two pieces, the two halves being joined together over the centre line of the bridge. These shafts are 11½in. and 14in. in diameter, and have a bearing at the two outside, and at the two middle fixed girders, they pass through the remaining girders but are not supported by them—Fig. 86, Plate V.

At the end of the leaf on the south pier, hydraulic cylinders are attached for working the locking bolts which fix the two leaves together when the bridge is closed. There are four of these cylinders, each being placed between the webs of the main girders. The bolts for connecting the leaves together are 5in. diameter.

There are two hydraulic lifts at each of the piers to enable pedestrians to cross the river at any time during the day when the bridge is opened for the river traffic, by conveying them from the lower roadway to the high-level footways and vice versâ. The entrances to these lifts are at the east and west sides of the towers. Each of the cages is about 14ft. long by 5½ft. wide and 9ft. in height, and it is proposed that they shall make twenty-five journeys each way every hour. Each cage is suspended by six steel ropes, four of which are 8¾in., and the two remaining ones 2¾in. in circumference. All these ropes pass over pulleys 4½ft. in diameter, fixed immediately over the cages, the two lighter ropes being then connected to leaden weights, capable of moving in a vertical direction for the purpose of balancing the empty cage. The four larger ropes pass round 3ft. pulleys fixed at each end of two hydraulic rams, which are placed in an upright position. These rams are 10in. in diameter.

It will be seen in these lifts, as in all other parts of the hydraulic work, that everything is in duplicate, so that no delay or accident could occur through any failure of the machinery. Mr. Gass was the foreman in charge of the erection of the hydraulic machinery at the site.

It remains to be seen how the shipping will accommodate itself to these new conditions. There is, however, no doubt that the bridge can be opened and shut as quickly, if not quicker, than any moving bridge that is yet constructed.

THE MASONRY SUPERSTRUCTURE.

When the piers and abutments were completed up to a height of 4ft. above Trinity high-water mark, by Mr. John Jackson, the contractor for the foundations, a contract was let to Messrs. Perry and Co. to build the masonry work of the superstructure above this level. This contract included finishing the piers and abutments, as well as constructing the masonry towers over them. A subsequent contract was also let to Messrs. Perry and Co. for the formation of the roadway along the approaches and side spans of the bridge, as well as carrying out the arrangements for lighting the structure throughout by gas. The contractors were represented at the site by Mr. Wheatley, who had entire charge of carrying out the

The towers over the Middlesex and Surrey abutments have been built in the form of gateway towers not unlike those which guarded the approach to old London Bridge —Figs. 81 and 82, page 97. They differ slightly in character and general dimensions, that at the northern

turret containing a stone staircase, which communicates with the upper rooms and roof. The arch is ornamented on each face with bold mouldings, and its soffit is further ornamented with ribs, which at intervals form lozenges— Fig. 83, page 101.

panel is a scroll with the motto, "*Domine dirige nos.*" The string forming the lower member of the parapet is carried round the turrets, with gargoyles at the angles. The whole is surmounted by a high-pitched wooden roof, covered with slates, and having two dormers

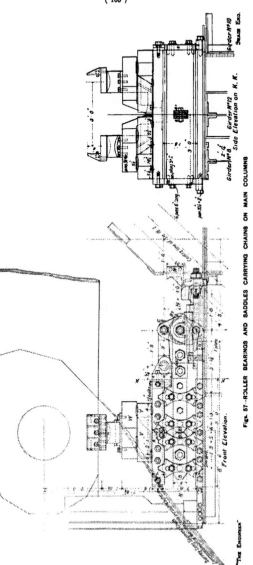

"THE ENGINEER"

Front Elevation.

Girder N°8. Girder N°12. Girder N°10.

BEAM END. Side Elevation on K.K. SHAM END.

Fig. 57.—ROLLER BEARINGS AND SADDLES CARRYING CHAINS ON MAIN COLUMNS

entrance to the bridge being rather the smaller of the two. The tower over the Middlesex abutment consists of an oblong building 74ft. in total width and 26ft. in depth, the road passing through an arch of 50ft. span. At the north-west angle there is a circular

The parapet is embattled throughout, and carried round the turrets at the angles at a slightly higher level. In the centre on each face is a large panel, surrounded by a crocketed gable, and flanked by pinnacles, containing the arms of the City, with its supporters. In a lower

on either face, and a lead ridge with finials at each end.

The Surrey abutment tower has a frontage of 90ft.; the depth, however, being the same as that on the Middlesex side of the river. There is also a slightly different arrange-

CPSIA information can be obtained at www.ICGtesting.com
Printed in the USA
LVOW08s1841070814

398029LV00001B/141/P